TRUTHFORLIFE®

THE BIBLE-TEACHING MINISTRY OF **ALISTAIR BEGG**

The mission of Truth For Life is to teach the Bible with clarity and relevance so that unbelievers will be converted, believers will be established, and local churches will be strengthened.

Daily Program

Each day, Truth For Life distributes the Bible teaching of Alistair Begg across the U.S. and in several locations outside of the U.S. through 2,000 radio outlets. To find a radio station near you, visit **truthforlife.org/ stationfinder**.

Free Teaching

The daily program, and Truth For Life's entire teaching library of over 3,000 Bible-teaching messages, can be accessed for free online at **truthforlife.org** and through Truth For Life's mobile app, which can be download for free from your app store.

At-Cost Resources

Books and audio studies from Alistair Begg are available for purchase at cost, with no markup. Visit **truthforlife.org/store**.

Where to Begin?

If you're new to Truth For Life and would like to know where to begin listening and learning, find starting point suggestions at **truthforlife.org/firststep**. For a full list of ways to connect with Truth For Life, visit **truthforlife.org/subscribe**.

Contact Truth For Life

P.O. Box 398000 Cleveland, Ohio 44139

phone 1 (888) 588-7884   **email** letters@truthforlife.org **truthforlife.org**

REMADE

REMADE

Embracing Your Complete Identity
in Christ

PAUL TAUTGES

PUBLISHING
P.O. BOX 817 • PHILLIPSBURG • NEW JERSEY 08865-0817

To founding pastor Armand Tiffe, my fellow elders, and my brothers and sisters in Christ at Cornerstone Community Church in Mayfield Heights, Ohio. It is a joy to grow in grace together with you.

Cover design by Jelena Mirkovic

ISBN: 978-1-62995-236-9 (hbk)
ISBN: 978-1-62995-237-6 (ePub)

Printed in the United States of America

Library of Congress Control Number: 2023947471

CONTENTS

Contents

SINNER: RESTING IN YOUR PROVISION IN CHRIST

SUFFERER: SUBMITTING TO YOUR PURIFICATION IN CHRIST

INTRODUCTION

1. A Triple Lens

*And we all, with unveiled face, beholding the glory of the
Lord, are being transformed into the same image from one
degree of glory to another. For this comes from the Lord who
is the Spirit. (2 Cor. 3:18)*

Each one of my adult children has a three-lens camera built into
their phone. The multiple lenses work simultaneously, enabling
the photographer to zoom in on a baby's adorable face, get a wide-
angled view of an ocean sunset, capture better images in low-light
conditions, and increase depth of field. The combined work of
these lenses enhances photo quality and results in a sharper image.

In a similar way, focusing on our Christian identity through
three lenses—those of saint, sinner, and sufferer—gives a clearer
and more comprehensive picture of who we are and what God is
up to as he works out his good purpose for us in Christ.

The Scripture above clarifies that God's purpose for every
believer ("we all") is to be conformed to the likeness of Christ by
beholding the One into whose image we are being transformed. This
is key to our spiritual growth. As we focus on the Lord, we are pro-
gressively changed, "from one degree of glory to another," into "the

same image": the image of Christ. The Spirit is working to transform every believer in a process called *sanctification*, which is the clearly stated will of God (see Rom. 8:29; Col. 3:10). This inside-out work, accomplished by "the Lord who is the Spirit," nonetheless requires our active participation. We must keep on beholding!

When we look at our identity through the lenses of saint, sinner, and sufferer, then our understanding of ourselves, our sin, and our circumstances will align with God's view, which is revealed in Scripture. As a result, we will become more secure in our standing before God, strengthened in our battle against indwelling sin, and steadfast in our suffering.

This triple-lens perspective is superior to a single-lens view.

If you look at yourself *only* through the sinner lens, it's likely you'll feel defeated by your daily struggle against temptation. You may lose sight of the reality that, in Christ, you have been raised up with the One who already conquered sin, death, and the devil, and you may consequently forget that you can persevere in the Spirit and walk in newness of life (see Rom. 6:4; Col. 3:1–10).

If you peer through *only* the lens of your exalted position as a saint, then you may begin to think you are stronger than you really are, even invincible! You may forget you are a fellow struggler on the road to holiness alongside those who are ensnared by sin, and you may fail to remember the warning "Keep watch on yourself, lest you too be tempted" (Gal. 6:1).

If you think of yourself *only* as a sufferer, then you may fall prey to the crippling power of victimhood. You may begin to see yourself as a passive pawn on the chessboard of life instead of as an active worshipper of your good and sovereign God, who is always working out his wise purposes for your good and his glory.

In this book, I aim to help you to look through all three lenses at your identity, to help you to take a biblical "selfie," so that your heart soars in joyful worship of the Savior in whose image you are being remade.

TALK TO YOURSELF. Which of the three lenses do you tend to look at yourself through—perhaps almost exclusively? How might that distort how you understand your relationship to the Lord? (It's OK if you don't know how to answer this question yet.)

TALK TO GOD. Ask the Lord to use the Scriptures and counsel in this book to develop and round out your understanding of Christian identity, so that you may experience steady progress toward God's goal of remaking you in the image of Christ.

TALK TO OTHERS. If this threefold lens is a new perspective for you, consider going to a wise Christian and asking them to teach and mentor you in your faith.

SAINT

PRACTICING YOUR POSITION IN CHRIST

The purpose of this first part is to help you to begin to look at yourself through the *largest* of the three lenses: *your standing before God in Christ*. Your first and primary identity as a Christian is firmly rooted in your union with Christ. Every other part of your identity is secondary to this. Mike Emlet makes this point so well: "We are saints who suffer. We are saints who sin. But we are saints nonetheless at our core."[1]

In this part, you will learn what it means to be *in Christ* and how to begin to practice your new position—that is, to see what it might look like for you to apply the fact of your union with Christ to your everyday life.

---

1. Michael R. Emlet, *Saints, Sufferers, and Sinners: Loving Others as God Loves Us* (Greensboro, NC: New Growth Press, 2021), 26.

A NEW IDENTITY

2. You Are a Saint by Calling

To the church of God that is in Corinth, to those sanctified in Christ Jesus, called to be saints together with all those who in every place call upon the name of our Lord Jesus Christ. (1 Cor. 1:2)

In the religious tradition I grew up in, a saint is a deceased person whose earthly life of sacrifice and devotion to God is officially recognized by the church and whose name is venerated. You might imagine how surprised I was when I learned that every Christian is already a saint. I'll be honest, it took a little while for this truth to sink in. Perhaps this is news to you as well. But this teaching is foundational to our understanding of our identity in Christ.

Today's Scripture highlights this truth: we are saints by calling. The word *saints* comes from the Greek word meaning "holy ones." To be a saint is to be set apart. Christians don't become saints through some super-sacred monastic lifestyle or by climbing the ladder of religious hierarchy. We are "called to be saints." It's our position before God from the moment of conversion onward. We have been "sanctified in Christ Jesus." *Sanctified* is also from the root word meaning "holy" or "set apart to God."

Like the believers at Corinth, however, we don't always behave like saints. Sadly, at times we think and act more like the world around us than like the God who saved us. Therefore, the challenge that lies before us as Christians is to put into practice our position in Christ—to become who we already are in our standing before God.

You are a saint. God has set you apart for his particular use. He has called you to live as one of his holy ones while remaining in a world that is not always friendly toward those who follow Christ. By living this way, you reflect his holiness.

Be encouraged to know that Jesus prayed about this. "I do not ask that you take them out of the world, but that you keep them from the evil one. They are not of the world, just as I am not of the world. Sanctify them in the truth; your word is truth" (John 17:15–17). Jesus prayed for your sanctification then, and he prays for you now (see Heb. 7:25).

Your sanctification is threefold. First, it is *positional*: God is calling you to himself (see Gal. 1:6). Second, it is *progressive*: the Holy Spirit works continually to empower your daily battle against indwelling sin as he conforms you to the image of Christ (see 2 Cor. 3:18; Col. 3:10). Third, your sanctification is *ultimate*: one day, you will be completely sanctified, or glorified (see 1 John 3:2). According to Scripture, God saved you to impart his holiness to you: "This is the will of God, your sanctification" (1 Thess. 4:3). You now walk on Sanctification Road.

Jesus called you out of the world to live in the world but without being of the world (see John 17:11, 14–15). The Spirit performs this sanctifying work through the Word, which Jesus says "is truth" (John 17:17). And take heart—today's verse also reassures you that you are not alone in this calling. You are part of a community of saints, the church. You are a saint "together with all those who in every place call upon the name of our Lord Jesus Christ." We, the church, are called out of the world but left in the world as a light and testimony to the sanctifying power of Christ.

TALK TO YOURSELF. The primary instrument that the Spirit uses to sanctify you is the Word of God. What place does Scripture currently occupy in your daily and weekly schedule?

TALK TO GOD. Take a few minutes to thank God for calling you to himself through the gospel and for providing you with his Scriptures in your own language.

TALK TO OTHERS. Discuss threefold sanctification with another believer. Ask them to share key lessons they've learned on Sanctification Road.

3. You Are a Work in Progress

And I am sure of this, that he who began a good work in you
will bring it to completion at the day of Jesus Christ.
(Phil. 1:6)

"I reviewed the results of your brain scan. There's evidence that you had a very small stroke." I stopped. I read the opening sentences of my doctor's email several times . . . and then read on. "It took place in the part of your brain that controls balance and coordination, and is what we call a 'silent stroke,' which means you never knew you had it." I learned it was impossible to know when the stroke had occurred because I had not had a test done previously to use for comparison.

After months of appointments related to chronic migraines, this news was both comforting and troubling. I had had a *very small* stroke, nothing more; that was a relief. And it was *not* in the part of the brain that affects thinking and communication, both of which affect relationships and are necessary for me to fulfill my life's calling as a pastor and teacher. Still, it was unsettling. I'd had a *stroke*, and I didn't even know it! Could it happen again? If so, could the next one be worse?

When difficulties enter our lives and questions fill our minds, anxiety may seize control and lead us down less-than-helpful paths. Therefore, we need to take every stray thought captive and bring it in line with Scripture (see 2 Cor. 10:5). Today's verse is a powerful reminder that the God who "began a good work" in us—the work of redeeming us from our sin and conforming us to the image of his Son—is the same God who will continue that work. The apostle wrote these words to build up believers by assuring them of God's commitment to the process. Here we see our threefold identity.

First, Paul addresses his readers as "saints in Christ Jesus" (Phil. 1:1). This doesn't mean they've achieved some sort of spiritual plateau, that they've "arrived." The Bible refers to all believers as *saints*, meaning that if you are a believer, you are *in Christ*. You have been joined to Christ by faith, and God sees you in union with his Son. You have been set apart by God, for God, and to God. Your new standing before God is all by God's doing; it's all of grace. And it is a present reality, not something for the distant future. God sees you as a saint—now!

Second, though believers are set apart as saints, we continue to battle indwelling sin. Positionally, before God, you are a saint. Experientially, however, you are still a *sinner* in the process of being sanctified as you struggle to live righteously. Therefore, you must lay aside your pride to "count others more significant" than yourself (Phil. 2:3), and you must discipline yourself toward Christlikeness (see 3:12–14). Ultimately, you will make ongoing progress because "it is God who works in you, both to will and to work for his good pleasure" (2:13).

Third, you are a *sufferer*. It is "for the sake of Christ" that you "not only believe in him but also suffer for his sake" (Phil. 1:29). Suffering is expected. He who began a good work in you will surely finish it "at the day of Jesus Christ"—the day of his return. Until then, God wants to accomplish a lot of growth in your life. Suffering is one of the instruments he uses to develop Christlike character and strengthen your faith in him.

No matter what we experience in our earthly journey as Christians, we may be confident that God will use it all to nurture a deeper trust in our relationship with him.

TALK TO YOURSELF. Do you sometimes get discouraged that you are not further along in your growth as a Christian? Think briefly about what your life was like before you met Jesus.

TALK TO GOD. In a journal or notebook, write a prayer of thanksgiving to God for his promise to finish the good work he started in you when you first came to believe in Jesus. Even though you may not be as far along as you would like to be, express thanks that you are not still what you used to be.

TALK TO OTHERS. Read 1 Corinthians 1:4–9. Write a note or send a text to a fellow believer that points out one way you see Christ reflected in them.

SAINT

4. You Are in Christ Jesus

And because of him you are in Christ Jesus, who became to
us wisdom from God, righteousness and sanctification and
redemption. (1 Cor. 1:30)

The apostle is clear. It was by God's doing ("because of him") that
the Corinthians were "in Christ Jesus"—that is, they were united
with him in his death and resurrection. Salvation is all of God. We
are in union with Christ and set apart because of his grace.

A few verses prior to the one we read today, Jesus is called "the
power of God and the wisdom of God" (1:24). Another New Testament letter reveals that "all the treasures of wisdom and knowledge"
are hidden in Christ (Col. 2:3). Three fruits grow from our spiritual
union with him.

In Christ, you received righteousness. You need the gift of righteousness because no one possesses any righteousness of their
own according to God's holy standard. Yes, compared to other
sinners, you may appear to possess a degree of righteousness or
goodness, but compared to God "all [your] righteous deeds are
like a polluted garment" (Isa. 64:6). You have no righteousness
to offer God to atone for your sin.

The good news is that when you turned to Jesus in repentant
faith, you "receive[d] the abundance of grace and the free gift of
righteousness" (Rom. 5:17). When you stop trying to work for
salvation and instead rest in the finished work of Jesus, your "faith is
counted as righteousness" (4:5). This means your spiritual account
is credited with Christ's righteousness, which he alone is qualified
to give to you because he alone fulfilled the requirements of God's
law (see 8:3–4).

In Christ, you received sanctification. You are a saint by calling.
God already set you apart as holy and cleansed you by the blood
of Jesus. This sanctified position is so sure and complete that it

22

provides hope for every kind of sinner, no matter their sin. The members of the church at Corinth had been fornicators, idolaters, adulterers, practitioners of homosexuality, swindlers, and drunkards (see 1 Cor. 6:9–10). Yet they were not forever stuck. They were set free. This is true of you too.

In Christ, you received redemption. God purchased you from the slave market of sin with the precious blood of his Son (see 1 Peter 1:18–19) so that you might be delivered from the kingdom of darkness (see Col. 1:13–14). This is your certainty, since Jesus entered the holy place "by means of his own blood, thus securing an eternal redemption" for you (Heb. 9:12).

Why did God do all this for you and me? So that we would boast *in* him but not *before* him. So that, by our testimony, it would be evident that God chooses "what is foolish in the world to shame the wise" and "what is weak in the world to shame the strong" (1 Cor. 1:27). As the apostle delivers this truth to our ears, he echoes the voice of the Lord through the mouth of Jeremiah: "Let him who boasts boast in this, that he understands and knows me, that I am the LORD" (Jer. 9:24).

TALK TO YOURSELF. Say to yourself, "I am in Christ because of the gracious work of God. Therefore, the only acceptable way for me to boast is in the cross of Christ."

TALK TO GOD. Write a prayer of thanksgiving for some of the ways that God has rescued you from sin and is now redeeming your life.

TALK TO OTHERS. Boast in the Lord! Tell a friend about God's goodness to you this week.

5. You Are a Child of God

*Beloved, we are God's children now, and what we will be
has not yet appeared; but we know that when he appears
we shall be like him, because we shall see him as he is.*
(1 John 3:2)

More than a decade ago, I went to a counselor. I was in a deep valley of depression accompanied by an intense struggle with anxiety and sought help from another pastor and biblical counselor. Perhaps that comes as a surprise to you, but it shouldn't. Every pastor needs a pastor, and every counselor needs a counselor.

My counselor listened carefully and compassionately as I described my faith struggles and negative thinking patterns and other aspects of my fallenness—at least the ones that were obvious to me at the time. Then he asked me to open my Bible. "Read 1 John 3:2," he said, "and stop when I say so."

So I began. "Beloved, we are God's children now."

"Stop," he said. Then he asked, "What does this say about God and about you?"

"God calls me 'Beloved.' God loves me," I said.

"*When?* When does he love you?"

"He loves me now, right this minute, even though I don't feel it."

"*What* are you?" he then asked.

"I am a child of God. I am a child of my Creator and Redeemer. That is my identity. My ultimate identity is not father, husband, pastor, author, or counselor. I am a child of God. That is who I am."

Why did my counselor direct my eyes to this truth? He wisely discerned that my battle with depression and anxiety was largely connected to distorted views of God. These directly impacted how I understood myself and affected every relationship in my life. This concept was not new to me, as far as information is concerned. I knew it in my head. I taught others the same principle. But I had failed to see it in myself.

Perhaps the same is true for you. Maybe you continue to strive to be accepted by God because you fail to think rightly about him and about yourself. He has already accepted you *in* and *because of* Christ. You are already accepted (present tense, *now*). Since by faith you are forever united to Christ, your understanding of who God is directly affects your understanding of who you are and spills into every area of your life.

Many Christians have a significant gap between their theology and practice, between their intellectual knowledge and functional knowledge. Do you? For example, you may believe God accepts you by grace alone but function as if you're ultimately going to be accepted because of your own efforts. You may believe God is sovereign (he has all things under his control) but function as if *you* are the one who is in control. Why? Because you have not applied your view of God and his love to your view of yourself.

TALK TO YOURSELF. Renew your mind; align your functional beliefs with what God says is true of you *now*, at this moment: "I am God's child now, and what I will be in the future has not yet appeared, but I know that when Jesus appears I will be like him, because I will see him just as he is."

TALK TO GOD. Pray through Galatians 4:4–7, making each phrase personal to yourself as one who is now a child of God through the redemption provided in Jesus Christ.

TALK TO OTHERS. Talk to a pastor or mentor about the various "identity lenses" (such as that of parent, spouse, employee, and so on) through which you tend to look at yourself. These lenses help you to define your circles of responsibility, but they can get out of focus. Discuss how your primary identity in Christ helps to keep these other identities in their proper place.

A RIGHTEOUS STANDING
BEFORE GOD

6. You Are Justified by God and before God

*For our sake he made him to be sin who knew no sin, so
that in him we might become the righteousness of God.*
(2 Cor. 5:21)

Imagine for a moment that you are the richest person in the world
and you happen to notice an utterly destitute and convicted criminal. Would you trade places with him? Would you give up your
immeasurable glory for his extreme poverty and corruption? If
you or anyone else were to do that, we would probably consider
it the greatest trade we've ever seen. Yet, as great as that would be,
there is an exchange that is infinitely greater: Jesus's exchange of
his righteousness for our sin. This—and this *alone*—is the basis
for repentant sinners' righteous standing before the holy God.

When we trust in Jesus, God looks at us through the lens of
the Savior's sinless character and sacrificial work and declares us
righteous through our faith. This action, called *justification*, forever
changes our spiritual status.

Unlike sanctification, justification is not the act by which God
makes us holy. Instead, justification is a *one-time, legal event*. At the
moment of our conversion, the perfect righteousness of Christ

is credited to our spiritual account and, before the courtroom of heaven, God declares us righteous for Christ's sake. Another term for this exchange is *imputed righteousness.*

Today's verse is breathtaking in its display of God's love for sinners like you and me. "For *our* sake," Paul writes, "he [God the Father] made him [God the Son] to be sin who knew no sin, so that in him we might become the righteousness of God." Through no effort of your own, your union with Christ immediately and forever changes your status before God. God sees you no longer as an *unrighteous sinner* but as a *righteous child.*

When Paul writes that Jesus was "made . . . to be sin," he does not mean that Jesus became a sinner. Rather, God the Father imputed your sin to Christ while he hung on the cross. Then the Father judged Jesus in your place, as if he were the guilty one. When you trust Jesus as your sin-bearing Savior, the Holy Spirit applies the atoning work of Christ to you. God freely gives you the perfect righteousness of his Son *in place of* your sin. He then declares you righteous, treating you as if you had perfectly obeyed his law just as Jesus did. This is *the* wondrous exchange!

As a result, "those who receive the abundance of grace and the free gift of righteousness reign in life through the one man Jesus Christ" (Rom. 5:17). "Through him we have also obtained access by faith into this grace in which we stand, and we rejoice in hope of the glory of God" (v. 2). This is all of grace: "By works of the law no human being will be justified in his sight" (3:20); "we also have believed in Christ Jesus, in order to be justified by faith in Christ and not by works of the law" (Gal. 2:16). Jerry Bridges is spot-on when he writes, "In our standing before God, we will never be more righteous, even in heaven, than we were the day we trusted Christ, or we are now."[1]

1. Jerry Bridges, *The Gospel for Real Life: Turn to the Liberating Power of the Cross . . . Every Day* (Colorado Springs: NavPress, 2002), 98–99.

Nevertheless, your justification is inseparably wed to a living faith that produces works reflecting the glory of God (see John 15:8; Eph. 2:10; James 2:17). Justification leads to sanctification, which is a cooperative work we participate in with the Spirit of God and by his power. Later in this book, we will turn our attention more fully to this process.

TALK TO YOURSELF. Do you ever feel unrighteous? If so, what do you do? Do you tend to work harder to overcome your sense of guilt, or do you run back to the cross where true freedom is found? How often do you meditate on the security of your justification, which is based on the work of Christ?

TALK TO GOD. Ask God to increase your everyday awareness of your righteous standing before him in Christ.

TALK TO OTHERS. Remind another believer today of their righteous standing before God.

7. You Are No Longer Condemned

There is therefore now no condemnation for those who are in Christ Jesus. For the law of the Spirit of life has set you free in Christ Jesus from the law of sin and death. (Rom. 8:1–2)

Every Christian wrestles against sin. As a result, it is not uncommon for self-condemning thoughts to float around in our heads and for doubts to upset our hearts. On top of this, the enemy of our souls, the devil, takes advantage of our sin and doubt and accuses us before God (see Rev. 12:10). To combat these thoughts and grow in the assurance of faith, we must take up "the helmet of salvation, and the sword of the Spirit, which is the word of God" (Eph. 6:17). That is, we must deliberately speak God's truth to ourselves to prevent lies from seizing control. We must remind ourselves of how God sees us *now*, in Christ. That's what the apostle Paul does in today's opening verse: "There is therefore now no condemnation for those who are in Christ Jesus."

The word *therefore* indicates this statement is a response to what comes before it. In the preceding chapter of Romans, the apostle has confessed that his unredeemed flesh causes him to commit unrighteous deeds that his new self does not want to commit or to omit righteous works that now he wants to do. Consequently, he cries out, "Wretched man that I am! Who will deliver me from this body of death?" (7:24). How does Paul answer his own question? With gospel truth. "Thanks be to God through Jesus Christ our Lord!" (v. 25). Paul reminds himself that in Christ he is not a victim in his battle against his flesh but a victor who can rest in the assurance of God's love (see 8:37).

Condemnation is from a Greek word meaning "penalty." It's the word Paul uses to speak of the spiritual death that is the ultimate consequence of Adam's choice to rebel against the good command of God (see Rom. 5:16, 18). According to Scripture, in Adam every one of us is condemned since "sin came into the world through one man, and death through sin, and so death spread to all men because all sinned" (v. 12). However, in Christ believers need not fear a future penalty for sin because Jesus paid for it in full, and we received the gift of righteousness through repentant faith in the one who died in our place and rose again on our behalf (see vv. 15–17).

Therefore, believer in Jesus, when you sin, God does not *punish* you. He has already punished all your sins in the body of his Son (see 1 Peter 2:24). Instead, your heavenly Father *disciplines* you in order to restore you to close fellowship with him, remind you of the depth of his love, and train you in practical righteousness, which leads to more blessings (see Heb. 12:4–11). He corrects you when you stray onto self-destructive paths so that you are trained to walk in wisdom and truth. Unbelievers stand condemned already (see John 3:36), but if you trust Jesus as your sin-bearing Savior, you are forever secure in him (see Rom. 8:33–39). You are no longer condemned!

When we speak such biblical truths to ourselves, self-condemning thoughts will flee. The apostle John assures us, "Whenever our heart condemns us, God is greater than our heart, and he knows everything" (1 John 3:20).

TALK TO YOURSELF. Begin a "Who I Am" section in your journal. List as many identity markers of a believer in Christ as you can think of and leave a few extra pages so that you can return to add more.

TALK TO GOD. Choose one of the identity markers you wrote down and spend some time asking God to help you live out that truth in your daily life.

TALK TO OTHERS. Ask a mature believer to suggest to you more biblical identity markers that you can record in your journal.

8. You Are Unashamed in God's Presence

Those who look to him are radiant, and their faces shall never be ashamed. (Ps. 34:5)

For he who sanctifies and those who are sanctified all have one source. That is why he is not ashamed to call them brothers and sisters. (Heb. 2:11)

Here is one of the most surprising statements in the whole Bible: Jesus is not ashamed to call us his brothers and sisters. Wow! How can this possibly be true? How can the holy Savior connect himself to people who have so many reasons to be ashamed? Before we answer these questions, we need a basic understanding of shame.

Merriam-Webster's Dictionary defines *shame* as "a painful emotion caused by consciousness of guilt, shortcoming, or impropriety." It may also refer to a condition of humiliating disgrace or disrepute. Biblical counselor Sue Nicewander provides this definition of shame: "A painful [guilty] feeling due to the consciousness of having done or experienced something disgraceful ... the feeling of being caught doing something bad or ... of being seen while sinning."[2] She then quotes Ed Welch's description of

2. Johannes P. Louw and Eugene Albert Nida, *Greek–English Lexicon of the New Testament: Based on Semantic Domains*, electronic 2nd ed. (New York: United Bible Societies, 1996), 1:309, quoted in Sue Nicewander, *Help! I Feel Ashamed* (repr., Wapwallopen, PA: Shepherd Press, 2017), 11.

shame-consciousness as "being exposed, vulnerable, and in desperate need of covering or protection. Under the gaze of the holy God and other people."[3] Before God, who sees all our sins, every one of us is exposed (see Heb. 4:13).

Before Adam and Eve sinned in the garden, they were "naked and were not ashamed" (Gen. 2:25). There were no other humans to hide from, and they had no reason to hide from God since they lived in perfect fellowship with him. But when sin entered the world, so did shame. The shame we feel as descendants of Adam and Eve generally appears in two forms.[4]

- "I am bad because of what I have done." Personal sin produces guilt, and from guilt may come feelings that we typically call *sin shame.*
- "I am bad because of what other people have done to me." The sins of others hurt us in ways that can cause negative feelings we may call *provoked shame.*

Shame often results in our feeling inferior or unworthy—beneath others, undeserving of their love. But shame may accomplish a good purpose when it leads us to repent as a result of guilt over actual sin (see Ps. 51), deters us from sinning further (see Rom. 6:21), and fuels our perseverance as we serve God in this life (see 2 Tim. 2:15; 1 Peter 4:16).

Shame can be a gift from God, but it may also become a tool the devil uses to defeat and cripple us. For example, men and women who have experienced abuse or betrayal often feel ashamed. They may believe that the abuse was somehow their fault and that they should carry at least some guilt and responsibility for

3. Edward T. Welch, *When People Are Big and God Is Small: Overcoming Peer Pressure, Codependency, and the Fear of Man* (Phillipsburg, NJ: P&R Publishing, 1997), 24, quoted in Nicewander, 11.

4. See Nicewander, 13–17.

what happened. Typically, this is untrue, but the holding power of shame and its lies are real and may easily control us.

In the context for today's Scripture, we learn that Jesus had to be made like us in every respect (flesh and blood) to make propitiation for our sins. Jesus satisfied, or propitiated, the wrath of God by becoming the only acceptable sacrifice for our sin. Additionally, he is our merciful and faithful High Priest. In his humanity, he understands and helps us "because he himself has suffered when tempted" (Heb. 2:18). Jesus understands the temptation to let shame control you and let your sins and failures define you. But his sin-atoning work removes your shame.

Jesus assumed the guilt of your sins and died in your place. Moreover, his blood removes the shame that results from your sins and the sins committed against you (see 1 Peter 2:24; 3:18). Though sinless, Jesus was treated as if he were the ultimate sinner and experienced the worst possible shame (see Isa. 53:3; Heb. 12:2). When he offered himself in our place on the cross, he despised the shame of his humiliating death, took our shame on himself, endured it, and now takes it away.

TALK TO YOURSELF. Do you feel ashamed about anything in your past? Ask yourself, "Is this shame connected to sins that I've committed or to ways others have sinned against me, or is it a mix of both?" Memorize Psalm 34:5 to help you to talk back to shame.

TALK TO GOD. Ask the Lord to forgive your past sins and thank him for washing you in the blood of Jesus. In his mercy and grace, God accepts your humble confession, repentance, and faith in Jesus as your sin- and shame-bearing Savior. Thank Jesus for removing your shame. Talk to God about the ways others have sinned against you, and ask him to release your heart from any bitterness that may remain.

TALK TO OTHERS. If you are ashamed of something you did in your past or mistreatment you received from others, talk to a mature Christian about it and ask them to mentor you in your faith. You will find a few recommended resources at the back of this book to assist you.

9. You Are a Servant of God

James, a servant of God and of the Lord Jesus Christ.
(James 1:1)

Name-dropping is a popular way to impress others, even among Christians. To casually mention our association or loose acquaintance with a prominent person immediately enlarges our perceived worth or influence in the eyes of those whose respect we crave. James, the half-brother of Jesus himself, did not succumb to this temptation. Instead, he called himself "a servant of God and of the Lord Jesus Christ."

James was one of at least six half-siblings of Jesus, the biological children of Joseph and Mary (see Matt. 13:54–56). Though not a full brother, James was a blood relative of Jesus Christ. Yet James doesn't endorse himself as "James, the blood brother of Jesus of Nazareth, the Messiah; chief leader and spokesperson of the church in Jerusalem; defender of the gospel of grace, called an apostle by Paul himself," even though all of that is true (see Acts

15:13, 19; Gal. 1:19; 2:9). On the contrary, James works hard not to draw attention to himself.

The term *servant* would be better translated "slave." This is the literal meaning of the Greek word *doulos* and "indicates full subjection to the authority of another."[5] By referring to himself as such, James acknowledges that he no longer belongs to himself. He is owned by God. He is now the property of Jesus Christ, his new master.

But this was not always the case. Even though James and his brothers daily witnessed Jesus's perfection as well as his miracles (such as turning water into wine in John 2:6–11), they did not believe that he was the Messiah. None of them were converted until after Jesus was crucified, buried, and risen (see John 7:1–5; 1 Cor. 15:7). James went from a skeptical, unbelieving brother to a humble worshipper of the "Lord Jesus Christ," the Savior and promised Messiah.

For James, to be Jesus's servant superseded anything he experienced as Jesus's earthly brother. *Servant of God* was his new identity. The same is true for every Christian.

As a follower of Jesus, you are a servant of God. You are a *doulos* whose ideal attitude is described by Jesus in Luke 17:10 (NASB): "So you too, when you do all the things which were commanded you, say, 'We are unworthy slaves; we have done only that which we ought to have done.'" Walking in obedience to your new Lord is the logical outcome of your faith.

James takes this as his theme in his inspired letter: he argues with heartfelt concern that our faith is shown to be authentic when it bears godly fruit in our lives. This is consistent with the teachings of Jesus, Paul, Peter, and John (see Matt. 7:15–23; Titus 2:11–14; 1 Peter 1:8–9; 1 John 2:3–6). True faith produces obedience.

5. Kurt A. Richardson, *James*, The New American Commentary (Nashville: Holman Reference, 1997), 53.

You have a new master, Jesus. You are called to "no longer live for [yourself] but for him who for [your] sake died and was raised" (2 Cor. 5:15).

TALK TO YOURSELF. Your high and holy calling is also your identity. Think about it: you are a servant of the Most High God!

TALK TO GOD. Write a prayer confessing any areas the Holy Spirit shows you where you have not treated Jesus as your Lord.

TALK TO OTHERS. Share with a trusted believer what you prayed above.

10. You Already Possess Every Spiritual Blessing

Blessed be the God and Father of our Lord Jesus Christ,
who has blessed us in Christ with every spiritual blessing in
the heavenly places. (Eph. 1:3)

The doctrine of God's sovereignty will blow our circuits if we expect to fully understand it apart from childlike faith. It's impossible for our finite minds to comprehend his infinite ways (see Rom. 11:34). God is dependent on nothing and controlled by no one; he is self-existent and self-sustaining. He needs no one.

Yet his eternal plan includes us! Our salvation is such a wonder to behold that "angels long to look" into it (1 Peter 1:12).

The psalmist declares, "Our God is in the heavens; he does all that he pleases" (Ps. 115:3). His sovereignty, absolute power, and authority are forever wed to divine decrees that were issued forth from eternity. God is working in his world, and his magnum opus is the reconciliation of his enemies to himself.

Today's Scripture introduces the divine plan by blessing God. The Greek word for *bless*, from which we get *eulogy*, means "to speak well of." In other words, the eternal plan of salvation should cause us to praise and bless God—to speak well of him.

This expectation is not new; believers have been blessing God throughout biblical history. Isaiah writes, "From the ends of the earth we hear songs of praise, of glory to the Righteous One" (Isa. 24:16). The psalmist exhorts God's people this way: "Blessed be the LORD, the God of Israel, who alone does wondrous things. Blessed be his glorious name forever; may the whole earth be filled with his glory! Amen and Amen!" (Ps. 72:18–19). We should bless God for the marvelous works he accomplished for us. Praise is the acceptable response from those who are blessed with the grace of salvation.

The blessings God has blessed you with are *spiritual*. This is not in contrast to *material* or *physical* blessings but refers to blessings that flow from the Holy Spirit. Jesus promised, "The Helper, the Holy Spirit, whom the Father will send in my name, he will teach you all things and bring to your remembrance all that I have said to you" (John 14:26). The Holy Spirit applies God's truth to your heart. He regenerates spiritually dead sinners and then indwells each of us at the moment of conversion. In Acts 1:4–5, Jesus told the apostles to wait for the Holy Spirit to bestow on them the spiritual blessing of his power.

The sphere of these blessings is twofold. First, they exist *in the "heavenly places"* (Eph. 1:3, 20; 2:6; 3:10; literally, "in the heavenlies"). This is not a physical location as much as it is the state in which you now exist; it is the celestial region of activity where every believer lives. It is where you receive all the blessings of God. Second, these blessings are found only *in Christ*. Only Christ-followers may take part in them. Many nonbelievers are looking for something spiritual. They are trying to meet their hearts' needs without realizing that the only way to partake of true spiritual blessing is by being *in Christ*. The blessing of God's gracious plan begins with a blessed God who bestows spiritual blessings through the Holy Spirit as we are united with Christ by faith.

TALK TO YOURSELF. Say to yourself, "In Christ, I possess greater blessings than the prophets of old, and I know more about God's grace than the angels."

TALK TO GOD. The psalmist said to himself, "Bless the LORD, O my soul, and all that is within me, bless his holy name! Bless the LORD, O my soul, and forget not all his benefits" (Ps. 103:1–2). Spend time blessing (praising) God for your riches in Christ.

TALK TO OTHERS. Use the blessings God has given you to bless others today.

LOVED BY THE TRINITY

11. You Were Chosen by the Father

He chose us in him before the foundation of the world, that
we should be holy and blameless before him. (Eph. 1:4)

In its original language, Ephesians 1:3–14 is the longest sentence in the New Testament. It contains the scope of redemption from eternity past to eternity future and describes our salvation from the vantage point of the triune Godhead. We see here that the Father planned it, the Son paid for it, and the Spirit applies it. Today, let's think about the role of the Father.

The wonder of salvation is that God chose us; he picked us out of all mankind to be recipients of his redemptive grace. The verb tense of today's verse indicates that the Father chose us *for himself*, yet we are the beneficiaries. Paul reiterates this in 2 Thessalonians 2:13: "We ought always to give thanks to God for you, brothers and sisters beloved by the Lord, because God chose you as the firstfruits to be saved, through sanctification by the Spirit and belief in the truth." From beginning to end, redemption is God's work.

The doctrine of election should lead us to fall on our knees in worship to God for his amazing grace. For him to choose any rebels out of the world to adopt as sons and daughters is amazing—

much more that he would choose you and me. Think about four elements of God's gracious choice.

The *sphere* of God's choice is "in [Christ]." Election is inseparably united to the work of Jesus. In fact, Jesus refers to believers as having been given to him as a gift from the Father (see John 17:1–2, 24). Together, believers are the bride of Christ. God loved his Son from eternity, and his choice is inseparably united with him and his sin-atoning work on the cross at a planned moment in history.

The *time* of God's choosing is "before the foundation of the world," a figure of speech meaning "from eternity." Prior to the creation of the universe, God selected a people for his own pleasure and possession (see 1 Peter 2:9).

The *purpose* of God's choice is "that we should be holy and blameless before him." Since holiness is the purpose of election, it cannot be its basis. God did not choose you because you are holy. Instead, he redeemed you in order to remake you into the image of his holy Son (see Rom. 8:29). You were "created in Christ Jesus for good works, which God prepared beforehand" (Eph. 2:10).

The *motive* behind God's choice is love. He chose you *for* himself, but his motive looked *beyond* himself. "In love he predestined" you (Eph. 1:4–5). He demonstrated the depth of his love by sending Jesus to die in your place *while* you were still his enemy (see Rom. 5:8).

Now, from a human perspective, we may look back to the moment we decided to follow Jesus. However, we would never have chosen him had he not chosen us first (see John 15:16). Welsh pastor Martyn Lloyd-Jones sums it up well: "If God's plan of salvation were to be dependent upon man, and the choice of man, it would certainly fail; but if it is of God from beginning to end, then it is certain."[1] We were chosen in Christ before time began.

---

1. D. Martyn Lloyd-Jones, *God's Ultimate Purpose* (Grand Rapids: Baker Book House, 1978), 92.

TALK TO YOURSELF. Say to yourself, "I am not an afterthought. God had me in his mind before I was even born. I am loved more than I know."

TALK TO GOD. Worship God in prayer, expressing thanks that your salvation was his gracious plan, not yours. Thank him for being mindful of you then and now.

TALK TO OTHERS. Reach out to another believer to discuss the unmerited love of God that motivated him to save us.

12. You Are Redeemed by the Son

In him we have redemption through his blood, the
forgiveness of our trespasses, according to the riches of his
grace, which he lavished upon us. (Eph. 1:7–8)

To redeem someone is to free them from slavery by paying a ransom. That is what Jesus accomplished for us. "In him we *have* redemption." It is ours now, today. Redemption includes three basic concepts.

We are redeemed *from* something—that is, from a life of sin. We were born sinners by nature and quickly became sinners by choice. Until we were born again from above by the Holy Spirit, we lived as slaves to our sinful flesh. But when the Spirit made us alive, we went from being slaves to sin to becoming slaves to

God. "Thanks be to God, that you who were once slaves of sin have become obedient from the heart to the standard of teaching to which you were committed, and, having been set free from sin, have become slaves of righteousness" (Rom. 6:17–18).

We are redeemed *by* someone for a price—that is, by Christ "through his blood." The punishment for sin is death (see Rom. 6:23); "the soul who sins shall die" (Ezek. 18:4). God's righteous justice requires that sin be paid for—but not by just anyone. Nothing but the bloody death of the perfect Son of God would do. This was the price tag for setting us free.

We are redeemed *to* something—that is, to a state of freedom. Once freed, however, we are called to release our liberty to the Lord who bought us. When we are born again, we are taken out of slavery and brought home to God. "Now that you have been set free from sin and have become slaves of God, the fruit you get leads to sanctification and its end, eternal life" (Rom. 6:22). Jesus owns not only your soul but your body as well (see 1 Cor. 6:20).

The writer of Hebrews reminds us that "without the shedding of blood there is no forgiveness" (Heb. 9:22). But he also emphasizes the guaranteed sufficiency of our Savior: "When Christ appeared as a high priest of the good things that have come . . . he entered once for all into the holy places, not by means of the blood of goats and calves but by means of his own blood, thus securing an eternal redemption" (vv. 11–12).

In Jesus, you already have forgiveness of sins; you have already been released from your sin debt. "He has delivered [you] from the domain of darkness and transferred [you] to the kingdom of his beloved Son, in whom [you] have redemption, the forgiveness of sins" (Col. 1:13–14). This is "not because of works done by [you] in righteousness, but according to his own mercy" (Titus 3:5). It is purely because of "the riches of his grace."

God's redemption is so sweeping that it includes all "things in heaven and things on earth" (Eph. 1:10). All creation, which now groans under the weight of the curse, "will be set free from its bondage to corruption" (Rom. 8:21). One day, God's redemption plan will be complete, but we don't have to wait until then to bask in the splendor of what already belongs to us.

TALK TO YOURSELF. Say to yourself, "I am not my own. I have been bought with a price. Therefore, I must glorify God with my body" (see 1 Cor. 6:19–20).

TALK TO GOD. Write at the top of a page in your journal "I Am under New Ownership." Begin writing short prayers that reflect your new desire to glorify God with all that you are.

TALK TO OTHERS. Share what you wrote above with a trusted believer.

13. You Were Sealed by the Spirit

In him you also, when you heard the word of truth, the gospel of your salvation, and believed in him, were sealed with the promised Holy Spirit, who is the guarantee of our inheritance until we acquire possession of it, to the praise of his glory.
(Eph. 1:13–14)

Recently, the Lord enabled my wife and me to become homeowners again. Having sold our previous home for less than we owed, we followed the Spirit's leading to another church located five hundred miles east. Five years later, we had recovered financially enough to purchase again. However, we had to work extra hard at multiple jobs to save up a down payment, the portion of the loan that serves as the promise that we'll someday pay off our mortgage obligation and finish what we started.

Today's Scripture reading announces that when you and I turned to Jesus after hearing "the word of truth, the gospel," we were sealed with the Holy Spirit, whom Jesus promised to send after he ascended to heaven (see John 14:16–18; 16:7; Acts 1:4–5). This *seal*, or pledge, is a legal and commercial term that refers to a first installment. We apply the same concept to the use of an engagement ring, which serves as a promise of a future wedding. God has "put his seal on us and given us his Spirit in our hearts as a guarantee" (2 Cor. 1:22).

Therefore, when it comes to our eternal salvation, we have a down payment like no other, and we didn't even have to work for it! It is a gift of grace that we receive through faith. The Spirit of Jesus is himself "the guarantee of our inheritance," the promise of more to come. He is the *promise ring* from Christ to his bride, the church, assuring us that one day he will return to bring us home.

In Bible times, kings and rulers used a seal to close official decrees. A lump of hot wax was pressed onto the document and, while still warm, was stamped with the king's signet ring. Like the king's stamp, the seal of the Spirit signifies three realities: security, ownership, and authenticity.

The seal of the Spirit engenders security. In Christ, your everlasting life is secure: "He who has prepared us for this very thing is God, who has given us the Spirit as a guarantee" (2 Cor. 5:5). You are forever united with Christ. Nothing and no one can ever separate you from your Savior (see Rom. 8:31–39).

The seal of the Spirit communicates ownership. Jesus purchased you with his blood, and the Spirit sealed you for your ultimate redemption. Consequently, when Paul challenged the Corinthians to flee immorality and pursue holiness, he appealed to God's ownership of them: "Do you not know that your body is a temple of the Holy Spirit within you, whom you have from God? You are not your own, for you were bought with a price. So glorify God in your body" (1 Cor. 6:19–20).

The seal of the Spirit testifies of authenticity. By the Holy Spirit's work, you are secure in Christ. Thus, the genuineness of your faith is confirmed. Kent Hughes says it this way: "He has tagged us, he has left his mark on us in our hearts, and we who have the seal know it."[2] The Spirit marked you out as God's precious possession.

The seal of the Spirit assures us of our ultimate salvation. His presence guarantees we will one day receive our everlasting inheritance in Christ.

TALK TO YOURSELF. Read Ephesians 4:29–30. How does the command in verse 30 affect your response to the command in verse 29 and vice versa? Consider committing these two verses to memory.

TALK TO GOD. Have you been disappointed by your speech patterns recently? For example, have you heard "corrupting talk" come out of your mouth? Or untimely or ungracious speech? If so, confess this to God and ask for the indwelling Spirit's help to grow in self-discipline and love for others.

---

2. R. Kent Hughes, *Ephesians*, Preaching the Word (Wheaton, IL: Crossway Books, 1990), 45.

TALK TO OTHERS. Ephesians 4:29 commands us to speak words that will build up others and give them grace. Is there anyone you should talk to this week whom you have torn down with your speech? Reach out to them, ask for their forgiveness, and ask them to pray for you to grow in Christlikeness in your speech.

14. You Are Adopted into God's Family

In love he predestined us for adoption to himself as sons
through Jesus Christ, according to the purpose of his will.
(Eph. 1:4–5)

Early in 1984, God adopted me into his family by opening my ears to the gospel and applying its truth to my heart. At the time, I was a prisoner to sin and a spiritual orphan, but I didn't know it. Though religious, I did not know the Lord; I did not have a real relationship with God.

It all started one weekend when I was not scheduled to work at the group home where I lived and was employed. On Sunday morning, I decided to visit the church that my sister and brother-in-law had recently begun to attend. The simplicity of the gathering took me by surprise. There was exuberant singing, preaching from an open Bible, and congregational prayer. Absent were the fancy religious garb and ceremonial rituals to which I was accustomed.

Two characteristics of that church stood out to me the most: the people clearly wanted to be with one another, and they openly expressed love for each other and for me. Strangest of all, they lingered for almost an hour after the service to visit with one another. They acted like they belonged to a family, not a religious organization, and their contagious joy left an impression on me.

The following week, I responded to a welcome letter from the pastor and joined a home Bible study on the gospel of John. Each week the blinders covering my spiritual eyes were removed a bit at a time so that I saw Jesus Christ as never before. By the time we reached John 3, the Spirit had prepared me to meet Jesus alongside a religious man named Nicodemus. That religious man's encounter with Jesus became my own when, in the privacy of my bedroom, I cried out to God for mercy and forgiveness. I turned from the futile self-effort of religion to the only One who could save me from the power and penalty of my sin. And I was adopted into God's family.

According to Scripture, your adoption as a believer is rich with assurance of God's ongoing love and commitment as your heavenly Father. Spiritual adoption is *the gracious act of God by which he places believers in Jesus Christ into his family and gives them the full rights and privileges of mature sonship*. Adoption results in a personal, permanent relationship with God and a new status. In Ephesians, the apostle assures you that it was God's love that moved him to predestine you "for adoption to himself as [a son] through Jesus Christ." In Galatians, he makes it clear that "God sent forth his Son" to redeem you so that you "might receive adoption as [a son]" (Gal. 4: 4–5).

Picture a rich father who intends to share his abundant wealth with his son. However, the son is still a child and cannot receive the inheritance until he has reached adulthood. Though a son by position, he is functionally like his father's slave or household servant. We are not in such a situation. Rather, by our adoption into God's family we each received the rights and privileges of a full-grown heir whose name is included in the guaranteed inheritance.

God broke in at the perfect time ("when the fullness of time had come"—Gal. 4:4) and sent his Son to be our Savior. He did this "to redeem those who were under the law, so that we might receive adoption as sons" (v. 5). In Christ, God not only rescued us from the condemnation of the law but brought us into his loving family where we are meant to enjoy the full privileges of mature sonship.

TALK TO YOURSELF. How does learning of your adoption in Christ affect your sense of the love of God?

TALK TO GOD. Why not cry out to your heavenly Father right now with whatever is on your heart?

TALK TO OTHERS. Share your spiritual adoption story with someone who does not know Jesus yet.

15. You Are Fully Accepted in the Beloved One

. . . to the praise of the glory of His grace, by which He made us accepted in the Beloved. (Eph. 1:6 NKJV)

Everyone longs to be accepted. It starts when we're very young and continues throughout our lives. Our longing for acceptance prompts us to make all kinds of choices with the hope of being approved by others and welcomed into certain peer groups. Our longing for belonging motivates us to act, dress, and speak in certain ways so that we do not appear odd. But, as followers of Christ, we need to realize that the fullest acceptance of all—by the One whose acceptance matters most in life and death—already belongs to us because of the finished work of his Son.

In today's verse, the apostle says that God "made us accepted in the Beloved [One]." The Beloved One is the only begotten Son of God. He is loved by the Father and by all who rest in him for salvation. By faith we are united to Christ in his death, burial, and resurrection. By virtue of this new standing before God, we are fully accepted *in* Christ, *because of* Christ, and *for the glory of* Christ.

Jesus's resurrection testifies to the Father's full acceptance of his all-sufficient work on the cross for our sins. The demands of God's righteous law were perfectly met by the only One who could fully measure up to its standard. As a result, those who find Christ to be their haven of rest also find themselves fully accepted by the heavenly Father. They are adopted members of his cherished family.

When we believe that we are already accepted by God, we are freed from the fear of man—the pressure to please other people more than we please God. This belief also dampens our temptation to conform ourselves to the world so it will embrace us. Instead, we are free to allow the Holy Spirit to conform us to the image of Christ, which is our heavenly Father's goal (see Rom. 8:29). By resting in the gracious acceptance that already belongs to us in Jesus, rather than striving for a superficial counterfeit, we are set free from bondage to the opinion of others and able to obey the Lord with courage.

One logical application of divine acceptance is that we can heed the admonishment to "accept one another" in the same way Christ has accepted us (Rom. 15:7 NASB). This exhortation comes on the heels of an entire chapter in which Paul instructs us to refrain from judging or rejecting one another based on differences of conviction and application of Christian liberty (see 14:1–23).

Christ accepted you based on his redeeming grace, not on your ability to measure up. Your individual acceptance, however, is not for your benefit alone. It is for the body of Christ and the glory of your Savior's name. Sinclair Ferguson brings this home to our hearts when he says of his spiritual siblings, "If Christ is not ashamed to indwell them, I will not be slow to embrace them."[3] Your divine acceptance fuels your acceptance of other believers in the body of Christ, even those with whom you may differ on nonessential doctrines, and to do so "for the glory of God" (Rom. 15:7).

Our longing for belonging is fully met in the saving work of Jesus, not in any merit of our own. By embracing our full acceptance in Christ, we are empowered to embrace other believers.

TALK TO YOURSELF. Are you ever tempted to prioritize acceptance from others over pleasing God? In what ways do you see a longing for belonging in your life?

TALK TO GOD. Write a prayer of confession about the ways you seek acceptance outside Christ. Ask the Spirit to help you learn to rest in your acceptance by God in Christ.

TALK TO OTHERS. Think of a person in your church who loves Jesus but applies Christian liberty differently than you do. Get together with them to talk about what you have in common in the gospel.

---

3. Sinclair Ferguson, "Union with Christ: Life-Transforming Implication," (sermon, Desiring God Conference for Pastors, Minneapolis, MN, February 4, 2014).

AN OBJECT OF AMAZING LOVE

16. You Are Drawn to Jesus by the Father's Kindness

But when the goodness and loving kindness of God our Savior appeared, he saved us, not because of works done by us in righteousness, but according to his own mercy, by the washing of regeneration and renewal of the Holy Spirit, whom he poured out on us richly through Jesus Christ our Savior. (Titus 3:4–6)

"And Can It Be?" is one of my favorite hymns because it celebrates the mystery and wonder of salvation. It helps me to marvel over God's love for a rebel like me—a love so great that he would do everything necessary to reconcile me to himself. Charles Wesley captures this awe as each verse builds to its crescendo: "Amazing love! How can it be that Thou, my God, should die for me?"[1]

The Scripture above reveals a similar wonder that filled Paul's heart as he pondered the impetus behind the divine rescue of sinners. God's "goodness and loving kindness" stirred him to send

1. Charles Wesley, "And Can It Be?" 1738.

his only begotten Son not to condemn the world but to save us (see John 3:16–17). As we muse on this truth, we are humbled and guarded from spiritual pride that may lead us not to "show perfect courtesy toward all people" (Titus 3:2). It benefits our spiritual health to remember that we were "foolish, disobedient, led astray, slaves to various passions and pleasures" (v. 3) before God intervened and pulled us close with his kindness.

As Paul continues, he identifies three characteristics of God's loving-kindness toward sinners. First, our salvation is "not because of works done by us in righteousness." Instead, we are saved by grace alone, through faith alone, in Christ alone. Second, God saved us "according to his own mercy." He pitied our helpless and hopeless condition apart from Christ and came to the rescue. Third, he made our spiritually dead, unresponsive hearts alive together with Christ by the "regeneration and renewal of the Holy Spirit." As we heard the word of truth in the gospel, the Spirit regenerated our souls and brought us to saving faith. In his abundant loving-kindness, God took the initiative to save us, as Jesus testifies: "No one can come to me unless the Father who sent me draws him. And I will raise him up on the last day" (John 6:44).

Thinking back to our conversions, we may remember the spiritual hunger we felt or the steps we took in our search of truth. Yet Scripture compels us to affirm that we were convicted by the Spirit and drawn to Jesus by the Father who loves us so. Wesley understood this truth well: "'Tis mercy all, immense and free; for, O my God, it found out me."

TALK TO YOURSELF. Have you ever thought of your salvation in this way before? Tell yourself now, "Before I found Jesus, he found me. Before I sought God, he began drawing me."

TALK TO GOD. In response to the kindness of God that brought you to repentance and faith, lift your voice in praise: "My chains fell off, my heart was free; I rose, went forth and followed Thee."

TALK TO OTHERS. This week, in your church's small group or another gathering of believers, sing the hymn "And Can It Be?"

17. You Are Born Again to a Living Hope

Blessed be the God and Father of our Lord Jesus Christ!
According to his great mercy, he has caused us to be born
again to a living hope through the resurrection of Jesus
Christ from the dead. (1 Peter 1:3)

A dead savior cannot save anyone, but a living Savior can "save to the uttermost those who draw near to God through him" (Heb. 7:25). Jesus conquered sin, death, and the grave and now sits at the right hand of God. He alone rescues us from eternal damnation and gives us new life. Our salvation rests on this living hope, as does our ability to triumph over any of our difficulties in the here and now.

Writing to suffering Christians, Peter moves us from looking at our present trouble to hoping in the future fulfillment of God's saving promise. His aim is to shift our focus by reminding us that we are now new creatures in Christ because God has "caused us to be born again." The word translated "born again" means to be regenerated, to be born anew. It refers to the brand-new start we are given when God fills us with divine life.

The new birth is necessary since we are born into this world dead. Before Jesus found us, we were spiritual corpses, "dead in the trespasses and sins in which [we] once walked" (Eph. 2:1–2), but God made us "alive together with him, having forgiven us all our trespasses" (Col. 2:13). For this reason, Jesus makes it clear that the new birth is required to enter the kingdom of God (see John 3:1–15).

In today's Scripture, the apostle gives us three reasons we should praise God for the miracle of the new birth.

The new birth is "according to [God's] great mercy." God's justice and love merged at the cross to fling open the door for sinners to experience his compassionate grace. Matt Papa and Matt Boswell capture this beautifully in their 2016 hymn "His Mercy Is More"—God's mercy outnumbers our sins. Our salvation is anchored to God's mercy alone, not to our own merit (see Eph. 2:4–7).

The new birth is accomplished by God alone. God "caused us to be born again." The instrument the Spirit used to initiate our rebirth is "the living and abiding word of God" (1 Peter 1:23). Scripture, empowered by the Spirit, produces faith in Christ (see Rom. 10:17). "Of his own will [God] brought us forth by the word of truth" (James 1:18).

The new birth activates an eternal hope. In the Bible, hope refers not to an optimistic possibility but to a confident expectation. It's not "I hope my favorite team wins the Super Bowl" or "I hope my spouse picks up takeout on the way home tonight." Biblical hope is the confident assurance that God will fulfill all that he promised in Christ. It is "a living hope" (1 Peter 1:3) that looks forward to "our blessed hope"—our Savior's return in glory (Titus 2:13). Jesus lives to save and keep on saving.

God accomplishes our miraculous rebirth "through the resurrection of Jesus Christ." At the cross, Jesus "was delivered up for our trespasses," but he also rose again "for our justification" (Rom. 4:25).

TALK TO YOURSELF. Read 1 Peter 1:3–5. How does the apostle describe your future inheritance in Christ? How will thinking about your inheritance encourage you to trust God in times of difficulty?

TALK TO GOD. Listen to the hymn "His Mercy Is More." In your journal, respond by writing out a prayer of thanks to God for his mercy and your new life made possible because of the resurrection of Jesus Christ.

TALK TO OTHERS. The book of 1 Peter was written to persecuted Christians who were living under the reign of the ruthless emperor Nero. Name a fellow Christian you know who is going through a difficult trial (perhaps because of following Christ). Send a handwritten note or text containing a brief word of biblically based encouragement.

18. You Are a Sheep

I am the good shepherd. I know my own and my own know me, just as the Father knows me and I know the Father; and I lay down my life for the sheep. (John 10:14–15)

Sheep get a bad rap in some Christian circles. "Sheep are stupid," I've heard more than one preacher say, "and that's why the Bible compares us to them." That's not exactly true, but domesticated sheep are weak and fully dependent on their shepherd to protect and care for them. Like sheep, we are completely dependent, and we tend to stray (see Isa. 53:6; Rom. 5:6). We need a strong and kind shepherd to rescue us from eternal danger and bring us into the protection and nourishment of his pasture.

Today's Scripture is part of a longer teaching passage in which Jesus identifies himself as both the door into God's sheepfold and the Good Shepherd who cares for all who enter and become his sheep (see John 10:1–15). Once we enter the sheepfold through repentant faith in Jesus, we remain under the care and protection of a Good Shepherd who has a close bond with each of his sheep. Think about two ramifications of this relationship.

Jesus knows you. When Jesus says, "I know my own and my own know me," he speaks of knowledge that is based on relationship. Jesus doesn't merely know *about* you or your needs, but he knows *you* . . . in relationship. Likewise, as one of his sheep, you don't merely know *about* Jesus, but you know *him* . . . in your union with him. When you turned from unbelief and embraced Jesus by faith, you didn't get a new religion. You got a new relationship. You know Jesus "just as the Father knows [Jesus] and [he] know[s] the Father." That's intimate! But like every relationship, the one you have with Jesus is not static. It's either deepening or eroding, moving forward or slipping back. Jesus knows you, but he desires for you to know him more deeply, to "grow in the grace and knowledge of [your] Lord and Savior Jesus Christ" (2 Peter 3:18). You do this by listening to your Shepherd's voice in the Word and talking to him through prayer.

Jesus laid down his life for you. The Good Shepherd offered himself as the Lamb of God so that you could enter the sheepfold of God. Unlike the thief who tries to bypass the door by climbing in "by another way" (John 10:1) or the hireling who flees because he "cares nothing for the sheep" (v. 13), Jesus is the faithful Shepherd who opened the door into God's pasture. The

Good Shepherd "calls his own sheep by name and leads them out. When he has brought out all his own, he goes before them, and the sheep follow him, for they know his voice" (vv. 3–4). So, when you feel threatened by the thief who "comes only to steal and kill and destroy," or by any other danger, you may rest your fearful heart in the knowledge that Jesus came so that you "may have life and have it abundantly" (v. 10).

We are sheep, and that is good news. Our Good Shepherd knows us, loves us, and protects us.

TALK TO YOURSELF. How does the imagery of Jesus as your Good Shepherd encourage you to trust in his care?

TALK TO GOD. Like Asaph, who led God's people in musical prayers, say to your Shepherd, "We your people, the sheep of your pasture, will give thanks to you forever; from generation to generation we will recount your praise" (Ps. 79:13).

TALK TO OTHERS. Ask one or two mature Christians to share with you some of the ways the Lord has cared for them as their Shepherd.

19. You Reflect God's Glory

So, whether you eat or drink, or whatever you do, do all to
the glory of God. (1 Cor. 10:31)

When I was a boy, most of my summers were spent riding bikes with my brothers and friends. Because we sometimes rode at night, my parents insisted that we fasten numerous reflectors onto our bikes to ensure that any approaching vehicle's headlights made us visible. The reflectors were not sources of light but simply mirrored any available light.

Such is God's intention for followers of Christ. We are lights of the world, but we are not sources of light ourselves. Instead, to the extent that we reflect Jesus—the true Light of the World—we reflect God's glory (see Matt. 5:14; John 9:5; Phil. 2:15).

As the apostle Paul wraps up his thoughts in Ephesians 1:3–14 about the partnership of the Father, Son, and Holy Spirit in accomplishing the redemption of sinners, he declares its purpose: "So that we who were the first to hope in Christ might be to the praise of his glory" (v. 12). Another way to say this is "We are saved to glorify God." But what does this mean?

The "glory of God" refers to the weight of all his perfections. Therefore, to glorify God does not mean we *add* anything to the perfections of God, but it means we *magnify* or draw more attention to him. Let me illustrate this another way: To glorify God means to take a wallet-sized portrait of him and make it look like an 11 x 17 wall-mounted print. Everything we do should enlarge God's glory so that other people's opinion of him increases. To glorify God means to enlarge or improve his reputation in our sinful, broken world.

You may ask, "What do you mean by *improve* God's reputation? God will take care of his own reputation." That's true, but only to an extent. One of the results of Spirit-empowered transformation is that we begin to reflect his character in every part of our lives:

"So, whether you eat or drink, or whatever you do, do all to the glory of God." In the original context in which Paul's admonition was written, some believers in Corinth were fiercely advocating for the full, open use of their spiritual liberties—even when they were aware it might harm another Christian's spiritual growth. The apostle challenges them to pursue the glory of God—not their own pleasure—as their highest goal.

As a follower of Christ, you are called to do all things in such a manner that God's reputation is improved in the minds of other people. God's reputation itself does not need to be improved in the sense that any change needs to take place in him. No, he is already perfect! He is the very definition of perfection. However, how others think of God needs to be enhanced.

In Christ, there is no such thing as sacred and secular. "Whatever you do, in word or deed, do everything in the name of the Lord Jesus, giving thanks to God the Father through him" (Col. 3:17). Everything we do is sacred. All things, therefore, should be done not merely for our benefit but to increase people's opinion of God.

TALK TO YOURSELF. In Christ, one of your greatest honors is to represent him on earth, to reflect his righteousness and mercy to a world that desperately needs to see a balance of grace and truth. How is your reflection?

TALK TO GOD. Ask God to help you to enlarge others' opinions of him. Take time to worship him right now.

TALK TO OTHERS. Tell a friend today one way in which God has enlarged your view of himself. In sharing with others, you will be helping them expand their view of his glory.

20. You Are Forgiven and Free

*He has delivered us from the domain of darkness and
transferred us to the kingdom of his beloved Son, in whom
we have redemption, the forgiveness of sins. (Col. 1:13–14)*

Every fifty years, God's Old Testament people were directed to
celebrate the Year of Jubilee. After seven cycles of seven years each
(forty-nine years total), the fiftieth year brought a time for rejoic-
ing (see Lev. 25:8–54). The name of this yearlong holiday comes
from the Hebrew word referring to "the joyful shout or clangor of
trumpets, by which the year of jubilee was announced."[2] Shouts of
joy sounded forth as prisoners were set free, slaves were released,
all debts were forgiven, and property was returned to its original
owners. Furthermore, all farming terminated for the year so that
the land and people could have a Sabbath rest. The old covenant
jubilee is a beautiful picture of the forgiveness and redemption
we find in Jesus.

In today's Scripture, the apostle Paul follows his prayer for
believers to be strengthened "for all endurance and patience
with joy" (Col. 1:11) with a jubilee, a triumphant shout from the
redeemed. The victory of Christ on the cross belongs to those who
are united to him by faith, with two notable results.

You are delivered from the power of darkness. The word *delivered* speaks of your complete rescue. In the New Testament, it
is used only in the context of God's saving work. Divine rescue

2. William Smith, *Smith's Bible Dictionary* (repr., Nashville: Thomas Nelson, 1962), 325.

emphasizes the horrific danger that every lost person is in. Before you and I were saved by grace through faith in Christ, we were totally incapable of rescuing ourselves (see Eph. 2:1). We needed Jesus to accomplish our complete deliverance through his death and resurrection, and we needed his Spirit to apply it to us at conversion. All unbelievers live under the tyranny of Satan. But the devil's license has been revoked for those who are in Christ. We are delivered from "the domain of darkness," that realm of moral rebellion against the light, as well as from spiritual blindness (see John 3:19–20; 2 Cor. 4:3–4).

You have been placed into the kingdom of Christ. Having been delivered from the realm of the devil, you have been "transferred" to a different spiritual domain, a kingdom "not from the world" (John 18:36). You have been set free from your old kingdom of sin and darkness and placed into the kingdom of the Son of God's love. This domain is marked not by tyranny but by grace. Satan rules his kingdom through fear, slavery, and darkness, but God rules his kingdom through his loving Son. Though we have not yet experienced the kingdom in all its fullness, it already belongs to us because we have become heavenly citizens and members of God's household (see Eph. 2:19; Phil. 3:20).

As a member of the kingdom of Christ, you have been set free from slavery by the payment of a ransom. You already "have redemption" because Jesus purchased your liberation when he paid your sin debt in full. And you are fully forgiven: God has revoked the penalty for your sin. As a member of God's household, you have been rescued from the family of the devil (see 1 John 3:10). Because of your union with Jesus's death, burial, and resurrection, God has thrown your "sins into the depths" of the ocean of his grace (Mic. 7:19) and remembers your sins against you "no more" (Heb. 8:12).

TALK TO YOURSELF. Shout for joy! In Jesus, you have a jubilee. Say to yourself, "I've been set free from spiritual slavery. My sin debt has been forgiven. I'm now included in the kingdom of Christ and the family of God. One day I will enter his everlasting rest."

TALK TO GOD. Write a prayer of jubilee that expresses your appreciation for the forgiveness that belongs to you in Christ.

TALK TO OTHERS. Share your jubilee story with someone who has not heard it before.

A FRUITFUL MEMBER

21. You Are Created in God's Image

*For you formed my inward parts; you knitted me together
in my mother's womb. I praise you, for I am fearfully and
wonderfully made. Wonderful are your works; my soul
knows it very well. (Ps. 139:13–14)*

Mankind was created for a reason, and every person has immeasurable beauty and value because "God created man in his own
image" (Gen. 1:27). And though sin "distorts the image of God . . .
it does not erase it."[1] Mankind is the pinnacle of creation. Created
by God as "male and female" (v. 27), we are designed to have a
relationship with God and others and to represent God on earth.
As creatures, we are fully dependent on the Creator to sustain
every heartbeat of our existence from cradle to grave. As persons,
we can plan and make decisions, and we possess the will to submit
to God or to rebel against him.

Our created and exalted personhood stirs King David's heart
to lift in praise and bow in worship. In Psalm 139, he mentions

---

1. Michael R. Emlet, *Saints, Sufferers, and Sinners: Loving Others as God Loves
Us* (Greensboro, NC: New Growth Press, 2021), 9.

four certainties concerning our value as God's image bearers that should lead our hearts to do the same.

You are a well-crafted work of divine art designed to draw attention to the Artist. He "formed [your] inward parts" and "knitted [you] together" while you were in the womb. In our mothers' wombs, God performs the most glorious work of crafting human beings, no two of which are the same. You are a unique creation of God.

You are designed to give God praise. "I praise you, for I am fearfully and wonderfully made. Wonderful are your works; my soul knows it very well." In Isaiah 43:7, God reveals his purpose for creating you: "Everyone who is called by my name . . . I created for my glory, . . . I formed and made." Even though you may not always be able to comprehend his ways, God is always up to something that serves your good and his glory.

You've been under God's watchful eye from the moment you were conceived. In your mother's womb, God carefully assembled hundreds of bones into the skeleton of a little girl or boy. These bones remained flexible long enough for you to be delivered. No wonder David cries out, "My frame was not hidden from you, when I was being made in secret, intricately woven in the depths of the earth" (Ps. 139:15). In darkness and safety, God created you while making your parents wait many months before unveiling his masterpiece—you.

You fit into God's grand design for the world. "In Your book were written all the days that were ordained for me, when as yet there was not one of them" (Ps. 139:16 NASB). Not only does your life have immeasurable value, regardless of your abilities or disabilities, but the day of your birth and the day of your death were ordained by God. Nothing happens to you by chance.

While we were in our mothers' wombs, we were fully dependent on God for life. We still are. And God's presence remains with us just as much today. "Where shall I go from your Spirit? Or where shall I flee from your presence?" David asks God (Ps. 139:7). These are rhetorical questions, of course. David couldn't go anywhere without God. Even down unknown paths, the Lord was leading him and holding his hand (see v. 10). God is our Creator. He was present with us every moment that we were formed in our mothers' wombs. We can be assured that the same is true even now.

TALK TO YOURSELF. Do you see yourself as a well-crafted work of divine art? Do you appreciate the ways that God made you different from others? Why or why not?

TALK TO GOD. Write a prayer of thanksgiving for being created in God's image, an object of God's love, and under his watchful care.

TALK TO OTHERS. Encourage someone this week by pointing out one of the ways God created them that makes you thankful for them.

22. You Are Recreated for Good Works

*For by grace you have been saved through faith. And this is
not your own doing; it is the gift of God, not a result of works,
so that no one may boast. For we are his workmanship,
created in Christ Jesus for good works, which God prepared
beforehand, that we should walk in them. (Eph. 2:8–10)*

Ephesians 2:10 must be one of the loneliest verses in the Bible.
Like I did at the beginning of my Christian life, many believers
memorize the two verses that precede it but leave out "For we
are his workmanship . . ." However, preserving the links in the
apostle's line of thinking clarifies and protects our understanding
of the doctrine of sanctification. It helps us to see that the new life
created within us by the Spirit necessarily produces good works.

Before you met Jesus, Paul writes in Ephesians 2, "you were
dead in the trespasses and sins in which you once walked" (vv.
1–2). Indeed, every one of us "lived in the passions of our flesh,
carrying out the desires of the body and the mind" (v. 3). *But God!*
Though we who are created in his image have turned to our own
way, we are now the objects of rich mercy. In love, he "made us
alive together with Christ—by grace you have been saved" (v. 5).

We delight in our rescue from sin and condemnation, which
is received by grace alone, through faith alone, in Christ alone:
"By grace you have been saved through faith. And this is not your
own doing; it is the gift of God, not a result of works, so that no
one may boast." However, salvation is not merely about going to
heaven one day to live with the Savior. We are also saved to glorify
God in the here and now; God has remade us "in Christ Jesus for
good works."

Yet you must remember that salvation itself is "not a result
of works." In other words, you are saved not *by* good works but
for good works. Consequently, it is not biblically accurate to say,

"Good works have *nothing* to do with salvation." It is better to say, "Good works have nothing to do with *obtaining* salvation, but they have a lot to do with *confirming* salvation." Righteous works are the supernatural fruit of genuine conversion (see Matt. 7:16).

Another way to say it is this: "Salvation is not *gained* by good works but *validated* by good works." That is, saving faith is a working faith: "For as the body apart from the spirit is dead, so also faith apart from works is dead" (James 2:26). You are saved by God's grace, not by your good works, "so that no one may boast." This guarantees that God receives all the glory for your redemption.

Yet you also need to realize that you are God's "workmanship," presently being acted upon by the Holy Spirit so that you complete the good works "which God prepared beforehand." Your salvation was planned by God in the past but is being brought to fruition now and in the future. This development, however, won't take place without your obedient cooperation with the Holy Spirit (see Gal. 5:16).

Progress that is made in Christ, even when it feels pathetically slow, assures our hearts that we belong to him. Glorifying God through good works is the circle in which we are now called to live, to "walk in." This is our new life in Christ, in contrast to our old life of sin (see Eph. 4:22–24).

TALK TO YOURSELF. How do you think of good works in relation to your eternal salvation? Are they the cause or the effect?

TALK TO GOD. Thank God that the forgiveness that leads to eternal life is based solely on his grace received through empty-handed faith.

TALK TO OTHERS. Ask someone what spiritual fruit they see in your life.

23. Your Citizenship Is in Heaven

*But our citizenship is in heaven, and from it we await a
Savior, the Lord Jesus Christ. (Phil. 3:20)*

A passport is a powerful document. It certifies our citizenship and gives us the authority and privilege to travel to foreign countries. With our passports we can visit other places as guests, although our citizenship remains in our home country. And, when it's time for us to return there, our passports guarantee reentrance.

As wonderful as earthly privileges like these may be, followers of Christ possess something much more valuable: "Our citizenship is in heaven, and from it we await a Savior." As you consider your identity in Christ, be secure in the knowledge that you belong to the kingdom of heaven—Jesus holds your passport. One day, at either your death or his return, Jesus will grant you safe entry into everlasting joy. Until then, you are called to live out your heavenly citizenship here on earth.

Today's passage comes from the book of Philippians, which Paul wrote to Christians; its message makes sense only to those who possess new life in the Spirit. Yet while penning a letter about joy in the Lord, the apostle confesses that he writes his words "with tears" (3:18). What has caused his grief? He is troubled when he thinks of those who "walk as enemies of the cross of Christ." Whoever these wolves are, their "end is destruction, their god is their belly, and they glory in their shame," all because they have their "minds set on earthly things" (v. 19). Their preoccupation reveals their god. This explains why today's verse begins with the little word *but*. Paul is emphasizing that, unlike false disciples who glory in their earthly status, "our citizenship is in heaven."

Later in the same letter, Paul refers to fellow believers as those "whose names are in the book of life" (4:3). The book of life is a record of all who have had their sins washed in the blood of the Lamb (see Rev. 21:27). Your spiritual passport into the kingdom of heaven does not contain a temporary visa, stamped with black ink, but an everlasting one, stamped with the red blood of the crucified, risen, and ascended Lamb of God. Your safe entry into the eternal kingdom is guaranteed!

We live on this earth for as long as God ordains, but this is not where our hearts should be. We "are no longer strangers and aliens" but "fellow citizens with the saints and members of the household of God" (Eph. 2:19). Our hearts should yearn for heaven.

TALK TO YOURSELF. Have you ever been homesick for heaven? Do you ever long for your real, everlasting home? How should your heavenly citizenship affect the way you live now?

TALK TO GOD. In what ways might you be living more like a citizen of earth than a citizen of heaven? In your journal, write out a prayer to God about the life adjustments you want him to help you to make as you consider today's reading.

TALK TO OTHERS. Read Colossians 3:1–3. How can you encourage your fellow citizens of heaven to set their minds on the things above?

24. You Are a Gifted Member
of the Body of Christ

*For just as the body is one and has many members, and all
the members of the body, though many, are one body, so it is
with Christ. For in one Spirit we were all baptized into one
body. (1 Cor. 12:12–13)*

God's design of the human body is nothing short of awesome. Six
hundred muscles attached to a frame of 206 bones are all kept alive
by seventy-eight organs and twelve working systems. If that isn't
enough to boggle your mind, then consider that there are approxi-
mately 37.6 trillion cells within these parts. Yet these myriad parts
all work together to form a functioning body.

In the same way, the church is a living organism that is sus-
tained by the life-giving Spirit. Paul describes it as a body made
up of many parts—all of which are indispensable as the church
fulfills the purpose of God. Six times in three verses, Paul uses the
word *one* to emphasize the union of the church body (see 1 Cor.
12:12–14). Some parts are weak and appear *less* important (from
our limited viewpoint), while some are strong and appear *more*
important (from our limited viewpoint). Nevertheless, each part
serves the purpose for which it is "baptized" or immersed "into
one body" by "one Spirit."

As members of the body of Christ, we must watch out for the
attitude that leads some to think, "I am less gifted and, therefore,
not an important part of the church" (see 1 Cor. 12:15–19). Pride,
even in the form of self-deprecation, hinders the body's functioning. Instead, humility reasons, "I may not have another person's

gift or strength. Nonetheless, I am a necessary part of the body and will therefore fulfill my purpose with contentment and joy."

But we must also guard against the attitude sometimes prevalent in prominent members: "I am more gifted and, therefore, a more important part of the church" (see 1 Cor. 12:20–24). Just as Paul offers gentle rebuke to those who think they are inferior, he corrects those who think they are superior. Pride, in the form of self-sufficiency, also hinders bodily function. Instead, humility reasons, "I need the other members just as much as they need me. Therefore, I will serve not from the platform of self-importance but out of a spirit of interdependence."

Both self-deprecation and self-sufficiency are unhealthy attitudes because they focus on self and thus will always hinder church unity. Through the Spirit's varied gifting, the church mimics the design of the human body. This same Spirit places both weak and strong believers into the same church body to complement one another. When humility reigns, there is "no division in the body" and the members have "the same care for one another" (1 Cor. 12:25). The strong care for the weak, the weak care for the strong, and God is glorified. What an amazing design!

TALK TO YOURSELF. Read Romans 12:3. Do you tend to think too highly of yourself or too poorly? Why?

TALK TO GOD. Thank God for his good design for the church and the perfect wisdom the Spirit displays in his gifts to you. Ask him to help you to grow in faithfulness and humility.

TALK TO OTHERS. Are there members of your church who appear *stronger*? Find a way to encourage them by pointing out how their ministry blesses you. Are there members of your church who appear *weaker*? How can you strengthen their hearts by expressing appreciation for them this week?

25. You Are Called to Be a Doer of the Word

Everyone then who hears these words of mine and does them will be like a wise man who built his house on the rock. And the rain fell, and the floods came, and the winds blew and beat on that house, but it did not fall, because it had been founded on the rock. (Matt. 7:24–25)

The Great Flood of 1913 was the greatest natural disaster in the history of Ohio, the state where I live. It killed nearly five hundred people and destroyed more than twenty thousand homes. When floods come, destruction occurs.

The same is true in the spiritual realm. Unexpected storms rage, and floodwaters rise. Those who have built their lives on a foundation of obedience to the Word of God endure in faith. But for those who have not developed patterns of obedience, life falls apart. That's the chief lesson we learn from today's Scripture passage.

The parable of the wise man and the foolish man concludes the most famous sermon that Jesus preached, the Sermon on the Mount. The men are alike in that they are both *hearers* of the Word, but only one is a *doer*. Here Jesus makes it clear that there are only two ways to live: either in wise obedience to God's Word or in foolish disobedience.

To fully appreciate this conclusion, we need a brief synopsis of the body of Jesus's sermon in Matthew 5 through 7. Jesus begins by introducing his main theme: the nature of saving faith. True salvation is birthed by the gospel and is accompanied by poverty in spirit and grief over one's sinfulness (see 5:3–4). When we recognize our spiritual and moral bankruptcy and humble ourselves before God to receive the King, ours "is the kingdom" (v. 3). When we mourn our sinfulness and turn to the merciful Savior, we "shall be comforted" by the One who bore our sins on the cross (v. 4). When we "hunger and thirst for righteousness, [we] shall be satisfied" (v. 6)—that is, we will rest in the righteousness of Jesus that we receive by childlike faith. Throughout Jesus's sermon, he calls us to be transformed on the inside as we live out our faith. This is the difference between the biblical gospel and moralistic religion.

As he winds down his sermon, Jesus gives several examples of two ways to live. There are two gates and two roads (7:13–14). The gate of discipleship is the only way to God—those who take it walk obediently in repentance and faith in their Savior and Lord. The wide gate, however, may seem like the easier path but eventually leads to eternal death and destruction. Saving faith is a working faith—it seeks to apply the Word of God to one's life.

On the one hand, obeying God's Word leads to security and stability, as when someone builds their house "on the rock." On the other, a life of disobedience is insecure and deceptive, like a "house [built] on the sand" (Matt. 7:26). Such a house cannot stand up to violent storms. Therefore, those who have "receive[d] with meekness the implanted word" should also "be doers of the word, and not hearers only, deceiving yourselves" (James 1:21–22). Doing the Word leads to stability of heart and mind while also producing a deeper assurance of the new work the Spirit is performing within you.

TALK TO YOURSELF. Read Matthew 5–7. Journal your observations about the differences between true heart change and outward moralistic religion.

TALK TO GOD. Write a prayer of confession to God that also expresses your desire to be more deeply changed from the inside out.

TALK TO OTHERS. Share your findings from the Sermon on the Mount with another believer.

A NEW CALLING

26. You Have Direct Access to God

Let us draw near with a true heart in full assurance of faith.
(Heb. 10:22)

Is it inconsistent for the Bible to teach that God "dwells in unapproachable light" (1 Tim. 6:16) while at the same time commanding us to draw near to him? If God dwells in the white-hot light of his holiness, how can sinners like you and me ever hope to take even one baby step toward him? If God is so pure, so completely undefiled, so sharply separate from sin, how can we ever come into his presence? He seems utterly unapproachable.

Yet the author of Hebrews strongly encourages believers not only to approach God but to do so with "full assurance." How can this be? Is this not impossible? It would be if it were not for one word: *since.*

Read today's verse in its context, considering its surroundings: "Therefore, brothers and sisters, *since* we have confidence to enter the holy places by the blood of Jesus, by the new and living way that he opened for us through the curtain, that is, through his flesh, and *since* we have a great priest over the house of God, let us draw near with a true heart in full assurance of faith, with our hearts sprinkled clean from an evil conscience and our bodies washed with pure water" (10:19–22). As we can see, there are two reasons you can enter God's presence directly.

You can approach the unapproachable God because Jesus paved the way to him with his blood. Jesus paved a "new and living way" into God's presence. As a result, you "have confidence to enter the holy places." How did he do this? "Through the curtain, that is, through his flesh." When the Son of God became man, he voluntarily veiled the fullness of his divine glory within the humility of human weakness. Jesus offered the veil of his flesh to be torn while enduring the wrath of God for three excruciating hours of darkness. By doing so, he met the righteous demands of the holy God and ripped the curtain of the temple in two (see Luke 23:44–45). By paying the death penalty for your sin, he threw open the door to God's presence.

You can approach the unapproachable God because Jesus is greater than all other priests. The author calls Jesus a "great priest" (Heb. 10:21) because he offered *himself* instead of bringing a lesser sacrifice to God. Jesus is the only priest who ever became the sacrifice as well! He "appeared once for all at the end of the ages to put away sin by the sacrifice of himself" (9:26). Only sinless flesh could satisfy God's justice and reconcile sinners to him; only absolute purity would do. As your High Priest, Jesus entered the Holy Place not made with hands to offer one sacrifice, one time, for all his chosen ones. As a result, God's holiness, righteousness, and wrath were satisfied. Three days later, God sealed and advertised this new access by raising him from the dead (see Rom. 4:25). Forty days later, Jesus ascended to God's right hand, where he now sits. "Since then we have a great high priest who has passed through the heavens, Jesus, the Son of God, let us hold fast our confession" (Heb. 4:14).

Jesus alone is the "mediator between God and men" (1 Tim. 2:5), who "always lives to make intercession" for us (Heb. 7:25).

Now all who come to Christ by faith may approach God with confidence because they do so through the Son's merit alone.

TALK TO YOURSELF. Are you sometimes timid when you pray? If so, why do you think you are not bolder? Read Hebrews 4:15–16. Consider memorizing verse 16.

TALK TO GOD. Write a prayer of thanksgiving for the direct access that you have to God's throne of grace, which Jesus opened for you.

TALK TO OTHERS. Share Hebrews 4:15–16 with another believer and spend time praying together.

27. You Are a Citizen of a Holy Nation

But you are a chosen race, a royal priesthood, a holy nation,
a people for his own possession, that you may proclaim the
excellencies of him who called you out of darkness into his
marvelous light. (1 Peter 2:9)

Knowing *who* you are and *whose* you are is vital to faithful Christian living. But that isn't true only in relation to your personal walk with the Lord. It is essential that we also apply this truth to our corporate identity, as we live for God in a world that is not always friendly toward those whose primary citizenship is in heaven.

Today's verse begins with "But," which announces a contrast. The first readers of Peter's letter were facing rejection because of their union with Christ, "the stone that the builders rejected [who] has become the cornerstone" (2:7). These followers of Jesus needed encouragement and counsel; they needed to get their bearings. They needed to be assured that, though rebuffed by the world, they were God's treasured ones. In short, they needed to know their identity; they needed to know *who* they were and *whose* they were.

First Peter 2:9 is so jam-packed with honorific titles for those who are redeemed by the blood of Christ—the true people of God—that it will take several meditations to explore their meaning and implications for us. But before we get to those titles, notice that Peter unifies his readers around their identity *not* as individual believers but as a community of God's people: the word *you*, in today's verse, is plural. As a fellow believer, Peter could just as well have written, "*We* are a chosen race, *we* are a royal priesthood, *we* are a holy nation." In other words, he wanted his readers to know they were not alone. What they were going through, they were going through together as a church. The same is true for us. We are not alone. We are God's beloved family. But what are some of our family names? We'll look at just two today.

We are "a chosen race." In today's culture, *race* is typically used to classify various ethnic groups, but that's not the way the word was used in the ancient world. The Greek word that is translated "race" may refer to a family, a people, a nation, or a generation. Peter is calling out *all* believers of *every* ethnicity as being a particular people chosen by God to receive the grace of salvation. On earth, this multiethnic community is a foretaste of the kingdom of heaven, of which the apostle John got a glimpse: "They sang a new song, saying, 'Worthy are you to take the scroll and to open its seals, for you were slain, and by your blood you ransomed people for God from every tribe and language and people and nation'" (Rev. 5:9).

We are "a holy nation." We are a community that is set apart by God and for God. Therefore, sanctification doesn't take place in isolation but is a family project. The more we grow in holiness, the more we bear "an actual likeness to God."[1] Our attitudes increasingly reflect God's loveliness, our thoughts his purity, and our actions his kind and generous nature. But the line between the world and the church is at times blurred. What is the cause of this lack of holiness—this disconnect between doctrine and life? Could it be that we have forgotten who we are?

We are an ethnically diverse people whom God has called out of the world to be his own. We are already holy in our position and therefore must strive "for the holiness without which no one will see the Lord" (Heb. 12:14).

TALK TO YOURSELF. Do you have the tendency to think of holiness mainly as an individual pursuit rather than a community endeavor? If so, why do you think that is?

TALK TO GOD. Pray through Psalm 86:8–13.

TALK TO OTHERS. Find a mature Christian and ask, "How has being an active member of a community of faith helped you to make progress in sanctification?"

1. Millard J. Erickson, *Christian Theology* (Grand Rapids: Baker Book House, 1983), 3:967–68.

28. You Are a Member of a Royal Priesthood

But you are a chosen race, a royal priesthood, a holy nation,
a people for his own possession, that you may proclaim the
excellencies of him who called you out of darkness into his
marvelous light. (1 Peter 2:9)

In the church where I grew up, I observed an awkward distance between the priest and the people in the pew. But the Bible presents a different picture. Christ, our Great High Priest, is not untouchable. He is not far away; he draws near to us. He is *Immanuel*, God with us, who tore down the wall of separation (see Matt. 1:23; Eph. 2:14). Now sinners like you and me may enter directly into the presence of God because Christ is our High Priest. Consequently, we belong to his priesthood: every believer in Jesus is a priest, including you, by means of the Spirit, who indwells the temple formed by God's people (see 1 Cor. 3:16–17; 6:19). Two truths help us to function accordingly.

Your priesthood flows from your union with Christ. The word *royal* in today's verse refers to the lineage of King David, meaning that your priesthood is forever connected to Christ, the son of David and heir to his father's throne (see Matt. 1:1; 21:9). The sacrificial work of Christ for sin, and in your place, is complete (see Heb. 10:11–14). But his ministry as Great High Priest continues, and your ministry as a member of his priesthood does as well.

Your priesthood involves serving the people of God. Earlier, Peter wrote, "You yourselves like living stones are being built up as a spiritual house, to be a holy priesthood, to offer spiritual sacrifices" (2:5). As a member of the royal priesthood, you are privileged to serve in many ways and to offer sacrifices—not dead animals, of course, but yourself as "a living sacrifice, holy and acceptable to God, which is your spiritual worship" (Rom. 12:1). You may also "offer up a sacrifice of praise to God, that is, the fruit of lips that acknowledge his name" (Heb. 13:15). Financial giving is also "a sacrifice acceptable and pleasing to God" (Phil. 4:18). And, as a priest, you can offer "supplications, prayers, intercessions, and thanksgivings" on behalf of all people (1 Tim. 2:1). All these sacrifices and more are made "acceptable to God through Jesus Christ" (1 Peter 2:5).

Perhaps you're thinking, "How is it possible that I am a priest?" Remember, this privilege stems from your union with Jesus. It's not dependent on you. Jesus did all the work necessary to bring you into a relationship with God. This relationship includes ongoing service.

Perhaps you're thinking, "I'm too busy to serve." But serving is not optional in the Christian life. Yes, at times we may need to step back or taper down for a season. However, it's inconsistent with our identity as priests and unhealthy for us and the body of Christ to make non-serving a habit. Like a pond with inlets but no outlets, our spiritual lives will become stagnant if we do not serve.

It's an honor not only to know Christ but to be part of his priesthood and, as such, to serve under him as our Head, leader, and Great High Priest.

TALK TO YOURSELF. Are you surprised to hear that you are a priest? Is thinking of yourself as part of the priesthood of Christ a new concept for you?

TALK TO GOD. Thank God for your high calling among the royal priesthood of Christ. Ask him to strengthen your spirit for service.

TALK TO OTHERS. Find another believer and read Hebrews 10 together. Discuss ways that Jesus's priesthood is supreme to all others, past and present.

29. You Are a Light in the Darkness

*The Spirit of the Lord is upon me, because he has anointed
me to proclaim good news to the poor. He has sent me to
proclaim liberty to the captives and recovering of sight to
the blind. (Luke 4:18)*

*Proclaim the excellencies of him who called you out of
darkness into his marvelous light. (1 Peter 2:9)*

While still an infant, barely six weeks old, the great hymn writer
Fanny Crosby was afflicted with an infection that inflamed her
eyes. When the family doctor could not be found, a pseudo doctor applied a hot poultice that burned her corneas and caused
scar tissue to form. As a result, Fanny lost all vision except for the
ability to distinguish between light and darkness.

Spiritually, we are all in the same situation by nature. Although
our God-given consciences inevitably teach us right from wrong
(see Rom. 2:15), we would barely be able to distinguish between
light and darkness apart from the illuminating ministry of the Spirit.

Opening the eyes of our hearts through the gospel is one reason Jesus said he was sent "to proclaim . . . recovering of sight to
the blind." In fulfillment of Isaiah's prophecy, Jesus did not merely
open the eyes of some who were physically blind but, infinitely
more importantly, came to open the eyes of hearts blinded by sin.
That's what the Spirit did when he convicted you of "sin and righteousness and judgment" (John 16:8). Then, by grace through faith
in Jesus, the Father "qualified you to share in the inheritance of the
saints in light" (Col. 1:12). You now have a light-bearing ministry.

On the day of Saul's conversion, Jesus said to him, "I have appeared to you for this purpose . . . to open their eyes, so that they may turn from darkness to light and from the power of Satan to God" (Acts 26:16, 18). You have a similar ministry. You have the privilege to "proclaim the excellencies of him who called you out of darkness into his marvelous light." The Holy Spirit wants to use you to shine the light of Christ that is displayed in the gospel so that he may open blinded eyes. As Jesus says to us in Matthew 5:14, "You are the light of the world." You are a light in the darkness.

TALK TO YOURSELF. Say to yourself, "In Christ, I have been called out of darkness into light by the Spirit of God. That same Spirit will give me boldness to proclaim the gospel to others."

TALK TO GOD. In Ephesians 1:18, the apostle prays for believers to have their spiritual eyes enlightened, so that they may know the hope of their calling. Take a moment to pray this way for yourself and a fellow brother or sister in Christ.

TALK TO OTHERS. Name an unbeliever in your life to whom you could "proclaim the excellencies of him who called you out of darkness into his marvelous light." How can you tell this person about your darkness-to-light story?

30. You Are a Redeemed Sinner

*Christ redeemed us from the curse of the law by becoming
a curse for us—for it is written, "Cursed is everyone who is
hanged on a tree." (Gal. 3:13)*

Have you ever redeemed something? Have you ever bought back something valuable that once belonged to you? What sacrifice were you willing to make to get it back? What price were you willing to pay to accomplish its redemption?

As we learned earlier, spiritual redemption was the act of God by which he purchased wayward sinners from the slave market of sin, freed us from the dominion of the devil, and brought us into his family. The purchase price was the life of his only Son (see Eph. 1:7). Peter reminds us of this ultimate sacrifice when he writes, "You were not redeemed with perishable things like silver or gold from your futile way of life inherited from your forefathers, but with precious blood, as of a lamb unblemished and spotless, the blood of Christ" (1 Peter 1:18–19 NASB).

Today's verse triumphantly announces that Jesus redeemed you "from the curse of the law by becoming a curse" for you; that is, by being cursed in your place. Jesus became the object upon which the curse was laid. So great was that first sin—the sin of the first man and woman—that all the earth was cursed (see Gen. 3:14–19; Rom. 8:20–22). Consequently, every man and woman was brought under the sentence of death and condemnation. Your sins—and mine—are such an affront to the holy standards of God and so diminishing to his incomparable glory that we deserve to be cursed. We deserve to be the objects of his righteous anger, to be sentenced to eternal damnation.

But God!

"But God demonstrates His own love toward us, in that while we were still sinners, Christ died for us" (Rom. 5:8 NASB). God so loved us that he cursed his own Son instead of cursing us. Jesus became a curse for you by willingly assuming your guilt and the punishment imposed by God's law. The law of God exposes our sin and thereby becomes our teacher, a "tutor to bring us to Christ" (Gal. 3:24 NKJV). The light exposes the darkness of sin and leads us to the only One who ever met its demands perfectly: "God has done what the law, weakened by the flesh, could not do. By sending his own Son in the likeness of sinful flesh and for sin, he condemned sin in the flesh" (Rom. 8:3). This he did on the cross in order to fulfill the law of Moses, which pronounced this judgment: "A hanged man is cursed by God" (Deut. 21:23).

By becoming a curse for us, Jesus forever changed our relationship with God and sin. So we sing, "Blessed assurance, Jesus is mine! Oh, what a foretaste of glory divine! Heir of salvation, purchase of God, born of his Spirit, washed in his blood."[2]

TALK TO YOURSELF. Consider the price that Jesus paid to free you from the slave market of sin. What was it like for Jesus to become a curse for you?

TALK TO GOD. Look back at the table of contents. Reflect on the titles and descriptions of your primary identity—that is, that you are in Christ. Journal a prayer of praise and thanksgiving to God for this indescribable gift.

TALK TO OTHERS. If you are reading through this book with a friend or mentor, schedule a time to meet up to discuss part 1.

2. Fanny Crosby, "Blessed Assurance," 1873.

SINNER

RESTING IN YOUR PROVISION IN CHRIST

In part 1, you learned what the Bible means when it calls you a *saint*. You are set apart by God, for God, and to God, but learning to practice your new position in Christ is a lifelong process. In part 2, we'll look through a second lens: You are a redeemed *sinner*—that is, you are a saint who still sins. Because Jesus broke Satan's back and unlocked sin's shackles when he gave his life for you, you can sin less and less and become more and more like your Savior. My aim in part 2 is to help you to grow in your appreciation for Christ's grace and God's provision and to better apply these gifts to your struggle against the sin that remains in you.

LIVING LIKE A NEW CREATION

31. Keep On Repenting, Keep On Believing

Jesus came into Galilee, proclaiming the gospel of God, and saying, "The time is fulfilled, and the kingdom of God is at hand; repent and believe in the gospel." (Mark 1:14–15)

Every coin has two sides, and this includes the coin of faith. Saving faith requires us to respond humbly to Jesus's twofold command to "repent and believe in the gospel." Repentance is the flip side of belief; we must not divorce these two concepts.[1] We cannot turn to God without turning away from sin. Nor do we repent and believe only when we first embrace Jesus by faith. At conversion, we turn away from sin to Christ and start down the road of discipleship. This lays the foundation of a lifestyle of ongoing repentance and belief: we must *keep on* repenting and believing.

Repent and keep on repenting. Repentance is essentially a change of mind, but, like belief, it involves the whole heart: the intellect, emotion, and will. Yet it is not the product of sheer willpower but the gracious work of the Holy Spirit (see Acts 5:31; 11:18; 2 Tim. 2:25).

---

1. For this reason, the New Hampshire Confession of Faith (1833) refers to them as "inseparable graces."

The word *repentance* comes from the Greek word *metanoia*: *meta* meaning "after" or "change" and *noia*, "to perceive." Literally, it means "to change one's mind or purpose . . . always, in the [New Testament], involving a change for the better."[2] Wayne Grudem defines *repentance* as "a heartfelt sorrow for sin, a renouncing of it, and a sincere commitment to forsake it and walk in obedience to Christ."[3]

Biblical repentance is more than regret over getting caught or sorrow over failing to meet God's standard (see 2 Cor. 7:9–10). It is a decision to turn away from slavery to sin in order to become a slave to righteousness (see Rom. 6:16–18). It is a constant necessity as the Spirit's ongoing work opens your eyes to the depth of your depravity. Repentance increases your desire to put remaining sin to death and firm up your faith-grip on the Savior.

Believe and keep on believing. Belief in the person and work of the Savior, the Lord Jesus Christ, is also an ongoing necessity. Saving faith is not a compartmentalized trust in God. It does not trust him only for future salvation and then lock him out of the here and now. Instead, having been set free in Christ, you are called to live not "according to the flesh" (Rom. 8:12) but according to "the will of God" (1 Peter 4:2).

The apostle Paul was so firmly convinced of his need for an ongoing faith that he made it part of his life's anthem: "I have been crucified with Christ. It is no longer I who live, but Christ who lives in me. And the life I now live in the flesh I live by faith in the Son of God, who loved me and gave himself for me" (Gal. 2:20). This should be your anthem too.

2. W. E. Vine, Merrill F. Unger, and William White Jr., *Vine's Expository Dictionary of Old and New Testament Words* (Nashville: Thomas Nelson, 1985), 525.

3. Wayne Grudem, *Systematic Theology: An Introduction to Biblical Doctrine* (Grand Rapids: Zondervan, 1994), 713.

TALK TO YOURSELF. Read 2 Corinthians 7:10. Make a two-column chart in your journal. In the left column, list the characteristics of regret. In the right column, list contrasting qualities of genuine repentance.

TALK TO GOD. Psalm 32 is one of the penitential psalms. Verbally walk through it, making it your own prayer of confession and repentance.

TALK TO OTHERS. Share what you learned from the 2 Corinthians 7:10 study with a fellow believer.

32. Behold, the New Has Come

Therefore, if anyone is in Christ, he is a new creation. The old has passed away; behold, the new has come. (2 Cor. 5:17)

To become a Christian is not to adopt a new religion or make another attempt at self-improvement. It's to be reborn from above by the Holy Spirit. You were a spiritual corpse, and, by the instrumentation of the gospel, the Spirit breathed new life into you. This is not the improvement of your old self but the start of something completely new.

Today's Scripture verse is a simple yet profound declaration of what the Spirit accomplishes in the souls of regenerate sinners. "Anyone" who is in Christ "is a new creation." When God made us alive in Christ, "the old … passed away" and "the new" began. By basking in the gospel sunlight of Paul's announcement and its surrounding context, we receive two rays of hope that draw us in a new direction.

New life in Christ produces a new, supreme love. "The love of Christ controls us," the apostle testifies (2 Cor. 5:14). A supernatural love for Christ has replaced your original love of self. His love for you, a lost sinner, has loosened the stranglehold of sin and turned your heart to love him in return.

This reciprocal love is not payback for his sacrifice. God forbid. Salvation costs you nothing. God already paid the penalty for your sin—sacrificing his only begotten Son—so that you could receive his grace. You are united to him by faith, your old life is dead, and your new life has begun—propelled by a new, supreme love for the One who loves you more.

New life in Christ produces a new, all-encompassing purpose. Jesus died and rose again so that "those who live might no longer live for themselves but for him who for their sake died and was raised" (2 Cor. 5:15). Your living-for-yourself-life has given way before a brand-new, overarching motivation—to live for the One who died for you and now lives again.

Paul says it another way in the book of Galatians, where he testifies of how in Christ he "died to the law, so that [he] might live to God" (2:19). Following Paul's example is possible only when you embrace the ramifications of the new life and from your heart say, "I have been crucified with Christ. It is no longer I who live, but Christ who lives in me" (v. 20). Living for Christ should now be the all-encompassing purpose of your life.

Conversion is nothing short of a miracle. At regeneration, the Spirit implants new life in us by means of the gospel. This begins an inner revolution, a radical change to our fundamental disposition toward God and his Word. What we once were has passed away, but in its place comes all that is new.

TALK TO YOURSELF. Biblical counselor Lauren Whitman writes, "God's activity in your life is not only to carve away what needs to go. He is also creating newness within you that will bloom and flourish for all eternity."[4] In what ways have you seen the old passing away and the new coming?

TALK TO GOD. What is one selfish desire of "the old you" that God wants you to wage war against? Make this a matter of prayer.

TALK TO OTHERS. Ask a mature Christian to come alongside you and help you to fight a stubborn besetting sin. Consider reaching out to a biblical counselor who can spend concentrated time helping you to focus your attention on this area.

33. Under New Ownership

Flee from sexual immorality. Every other sin a person commits is outside the body, but the sexually immoral person sins against his own body. Or do you not know that your body is a temple of the Holy Spirit within you, whom you have from God? You are not your own, for you were bought with a price. So glorify God in your body. (1 Cor. 6:18–20)

Today's verses were first written to Christians who were living in a culture not unlike ours. Corinth was immersed in sexual immorality. The city contained a temple to Aphrodite, the goddess of fertility,

4. Lauren Whitman, *A Painful Past: Healing and Moving Forward* (Phillipsburg, NJ: P&R Publishing, 2020), 62.

which housed a thousand temple prostitutes. Its reputation was so well known that to commit sexual immorality was to "play the Corinthian."[5] *Sex is for the body and the body for sex* was essentially the slogan of the day.

Thankfully, some men and women were saved out of their immoral lifestyles (see 1 Cor. 6:11). But they were still tempted by the flesh, as we are. Consequently, in 1 Corinthians 6:15–20, Paul urges followers of Jesus to flee sexual sin and gives three reasons.

Sexual sin defiles Christ's body. Paul asks the members of the church a question: "Do you not know that your bodies are members of Christ?" (1 Cor. 6:15). The answer is yes, they know it. Should they then "take the members of Christ and make them members of a prostitute?" (v. 15). "Never!" he says. Jesus is undefiled and always will be, but sexual sin defiles a believer's union with Christ. The one "who is joined to a prostitute becomes one body with her" (v. 16). The word *joined* is used of close bonds of various kinds, literally meaning "to glue." As a man and woman become one flesh when they are united *physically*, so Christ and the believer are in *spiritual* union with each other. We are in Christ, and Christ is in us. It should be unthinkable, then, for us to unite our bodies to others in immorality.

Sexual sin damages the human body. To "flee from sexual immorality," in the original Greek, is a habitual action. We are weak, defiled, and sinful, and we live in a sensual world. Therefore, when tempted from within or without, we must run for our lives like Joseph, who "left his garment in her hand and fled and got out of the house" (Gen. 39:12). "Every other sin a person commits is outside the body, but the sexually immoral person sins against his own body." Sexual sin is so deeply connected to the body that it harms us within. Commenting on this verse, John Calvin wrote, "*Fornication* leaves a stain

5. F. F. Bruce, *Paul: Apostle of the Heart Set Free* (Grand Rapids: Eerdmans, 1977), 249.

impressed upon the body, such as is not impressed upon it from other sins."[6] It may leave scars that last for years to come—however, no one's past is beyond redemption and inner healing.

Sexual sin desecrates God's sanctuary. Your "body is a temple of the Holy Spirit within you." The word *temple* refers to the dwelling place of God, the inner sanctuary. Indwelt by the Spirit, your physical flesh and bones now comprise a sanctuary of God. Your body is the Spirit's apartment. Therefore, you and I are never alone. We sin in the presence of the Holy Spirit. For this reason, Paul exhorts, "Do not grieve the Holy Spirit of God, by whom you were sealed for the day of redemption" (Eph. 4:30). You "were bought with a price." Hence, you are now called to "glorify God in your body."

Jesus died on the cross to purchase not only our souls but our bodies. We are not our own masters anymore. Our bodies no longer belong to us. We are under new ownership. Therefore, we must have the same resolve as Paul: "I discipline my body and keep it under control, lest after preaching to others I myself should be disqualified" (1 Cor. 9:27).

TALK TO YOURSELF. When you sin with your body, do you tend to think your body is the problem? Biblical counselor and author Ed Welch writes, "[The body] is the mediator of moral action rather than the initiator. In a sense, it is equipment for the heart. It does what the heart tells it to do. . . . It is not the source of sin and is never called sinful."[7] This echoes the teaching of Jesus (see Mark 7:21). Ponder the biblical truth that sexual sin begins in the heart.

6. John Calvin, *Calvin's Commentaries*, vol. 20, *1 Corinthians, 2 Corinthians* (Grand Rapids: Baker Book House, 1998), 220.

7. Edward T. Welch, *Blame It on the Brain? Distinguishing Chemical Imbalances, Brain Disorders, and Disobedience* (Philipsburg, NJ: P&R Publishing, 1998), 40.

TALK TO GOD. Write a prayer of confession to God, acknowledging your misuse of the body he created for you. Ask the Spirit to strengthen your resolve to resist temptation as you learn to depend on his power.

TALK TO OTHERS. If you have succumbed to patterns of sexual sin and need help to get free, reach out to a trusted friend, pastor, or biblical counselor. Recommended resources are at the back of this book.

34. Keep in Step with the Spirit

But I say, walk by the Spirit, and you will not gratify the desires of the flesh. . . . If we live by the Spirit, let us also keep in step with the Spirit. (Gal. 5:16, 25)

"The Christian life is not a playground. It's a battlefield." My mind's eye can still see the gray-headed preacher who spoke those sentences in a Bible college chapel in the late 1980s. Recalling his words has helped me to remain serious about pursuing holiness, while also prodding me to stay dependent on the indwelling Spirit of God. He alone is strong enough to enable us to win the long war against sin—and a war it is.

As followers of Jesus, we are commanded to habitually flee from sin and pursue "righteousness, godliness, faith, love, steadfastness, gentleness. Fight the good fight of the faith" (1 Tim. 6:11–12). Until we see Jesus face-to-face, we will always experience an inner struggle between righteousness and sin. Therefore, in today's verses, the apostle directs us to live under the influence of the Holy Spirit rather than the self-indulgent desires of the unredeemed flesh: "Walk by the Spirit, and you will not gratify the desires of the flesh." This biblical command begins with a word of contrast—*but*—that reminds us to look backward to find the context.

In the preceding sentences, Paul exalts loving others over expressing personal liberty. "Do not use your freedom as an opportunity for the flesh, but through love serve one another" (5:13). Since libertines abuse their freedom in Christ, by using it as an excuse to keep on sinning, they don't experience the same internal agony as the serious-minded believer. In contrast, Spirit-controlled believers walk differently because they think differently.

William MacDonald explains, "To walk in (or by) the Spirit is to allow Him to have His way. It is to remain in communion with Him. It is to make decisions in the light of His holiness. It is to be occupied with Christ."[8] To walk by the Spirit means to walk according to the ways of God, which are revealed in the Word of God, which is inspired by the Spirit (compare Eph. 5:18 with Col. 3:16).

The world, the flesh, and the devil will always push against the Spirit's agenda to remake us in Christ. Nevertheless, we must "keep in step" with him by being serious about overcoming sin and relying on his power. We are soldiers of Christ, but if we head into battle in our own strength, we will fail every time. So, be encouraged: the Holy Spirit lives within you to fight the long war alongside you.

8. William MacDonald, *Believer's Bible Commentary*, ed. Art Farstad (Nashville: Thomas Nelson, 1995), 1893.

TALK TO YOURSELF. Read Galatians 5:16–25. Ask yourself, "What work of the flesh do I need to focus on putting off? What godly fruit do I need to put on in the energy of the Spirit?" How does others-focused love help you to overcome sin?

TALK TO GOD. Now, pray through Galatians 5:16–25. Ask the Spirit to teach you to depend on his power to make progress in godliness.

TALK TO OTHERS. Ask a mature brother or sister in Christ to pray for you in one specific area where you struggle to walk by the Spirit.

35. Prayer Protects You from Temptation

Watch and pray that you may not enter into temptation.
The spirit indeed is willing, but the flesh is weak.
(Mark 14:38)

In *Sense and Nonsense about Prayer*, Lehman Straus writes, "No one can both sin and pray. True prayer will prevent us from sinning, or sin will prevent us from praying."[9] Why? Because prayerlessness is a subtle declaration of our rebellious hearts' imagined independence from God. It is a dereliction of duty and a failure to enjoy one of the greatest privileges we have as new creatures in Christ. The neglect of prayer may also expose a sense of self-sufficiency or laziness, both of which are unhelpful to resisting temptation. In

9. Lehman Straus, *Sense and Nonsense about Prayer* (Chicago: Moody Press, 1974), 24.

contrast, prayer demonstrates the humility of dependence on the Lord. A lifestyle of prayer keeps our hearts submissive to God and prepared for spiritual battle.

In Mark 14:38, Jesus tells us that when we don't depend on God in prayer, we will be more vulnerable to temptation—an independent spirit makes us easy prey. Rather than sleeping amid danger like Jesus's disciples in the garden (see Mark 14:37), we are to war against sin through prayer. One way we do this is by praying, "Lead us not into temptation," as Jesus taught his followers to pray earlier in his ministry (Luke 11:4). This ongoing prayer request guards our hearts from sin by keeping us alert instead of spiritually sleepy, sluggish, and susceptible to sin's allure.

In the book of Ephesians, Paul also teaches that prayer keeps you attentive to the assaults of the devil and his minions: "Put on the whole armor of God, that you may be able to stand against the schemes of the devil" (6:11). After naming each piece of spiritual armor, Paul identifies the posture of heart required for battling sin: we should pray "at all times in the Spirit, with all prayer and supplication. To that end, keep alert with all perseverance, making supplication for all the saints" (v. 18). Pray "to that end"—that is, with an awareness that spiritual warfare is certain.

Don't miss this: A significant part of your resistance to temptation and the attack of the devil is dependence on God's strength. This reliance is expressed most obviously through the godly habit of prayer.

TALK TO YOURSELF. What two adjectives best describe your prayer life? Have you seen a connection between prayerlessness and vulnerability to temptation?

TALK TO GOD. Personalize Jesus's pattern for prayer taught in Matthew 6:9–13. Here's one way to do that: "My Father in heaven, holy and exalted is your name. May your kingdom come, and your will be done, on earth as it is already being done in heaven. Give me today my daily provisions, and forgive me all my sins, as I continue to forgive those who sin against me. Guard my heart from temptation and deliver me from the Evil One."

TALK TO OTHERS. Call a brother or sister in Christ and ask how you may pray for them this week. Spend a few minutes praying with them over the phone.

BATTLING INDWELLING SIN

36. Does God Tempt Us to Sin?

Let no one say when he is tempted, "I am being tempted by God," for God cannot be tempted with evil, and he himself tempts no one. (James 1:13)

Only older generations may remember Flip Wilson's comedy acts, but the title of one famous skit became a household exclamation: "The devil made me do it!" Unfortunately, when it comes to temptation and sin, it can be easy for us to follow "Flip Wilson theology"—the devil gets blamed, and we get off scot-free. However, the blame game is not new; it's as old as Adam and Eve.

When God confronted the disobedience of humanity's first parents, they invented blame shifting. Eve blamed the serpent and then Adam blamed his wife *and God*, who had given him his wife (see Gen. 3:12). In a similar fashion, some of the first readers of the inspired letter from James took their cue from Adam and struggled with blaming God.

When God sent severe trials to develop their character, some followers of Jesus thought wrongly about God and blamed him for tempting them to sin. *If God hadn't let that happen, I wouldn't have* made those bad choices. *If God had given me a different spouse or better parents, then I would be in a better place today.* But James rebukes all who attempt to free themselves from personal responsibility by blaming their sins on God: "Let no one say when he is tempted, 'I am being tempted by God.'"

God is never the source of your temptation to sin, James tells us. The word *tempted* comes from the same word James uses earlier to refer to trials (see 1:2), but here it refers to temptation to sin. God employs trials to test your faith, yes—to strengthen and prove your authenticity—but he does not tempt you to sin. The holy nature of God forbids him from tempting you to sin for two reasons.

"God cannot be tempted with evil." God himself cannot be tempted; he is untemptable. It is impossible for God to flirt with sin, as other Scriptures testify. God is "of purer eyes than to see evil and cannot look at wrong" (Hab. 1:13). "There is none holy like the LORD" (1 Sam. 2:2). "Your way, O God, is holy" (Ps. 77:13). God is holy, unstained by sin. He cannot be tempted by evil and thus is never the source of your temptation.

God does not lead anyone into sin: "He himself tempts no one." When you are tempted, God is not the source. Your sinful choices are *always* your responsibility, ultimately. Yes, the devil enjoys tempting you, just as it thrilled him to tempt Jesus (see Luke 4:1–13). Yes, fellow sinners may provoke you to respond in sinful ways (see Rom. 12:17–21). But eventually, you and I are left to face the wretchedness of our own hearts. We have no one to blame but ourselves when we tiptoe around or dive into sin.

God is perfectly holy, untainted by sin in any form or degree. He is incapable of tempting us to sin. We must not blame him.

TALK TO YOURSELF. Are there certain areas of sin or temptation where you find yourself blame shifting, perhaps almost by habit?

TALK TO GOD. Have you ever blamed God for the consequences of a choice you have made? Admit this to God by confessing the specific way you have blamed him in the past, or are currently doing so, and ask for forgiveness.

TALK TO OTHERS. Have you been blaming another person for choices you made? Perhaps your spouse, a parent, a coworker, a former friend, or someone else? A helpful question to ask might be "Am I bitter or resentful toward anyone?" If you are, you may also shift blame to them. Talk to them about what the Holy Spirit has revealed to you and ask their forgiveness for ways you have shifted blame to them instead of assuming personal responsibility.

37. How Does Temptation Work?

But each person is tempted when he is lured and enticed by his own desire. Then desire when it has conceived gives birth to sin, and sin when it is fully grown brings forth death.
(James 1:14–15)

Fishing on Cowboy Lake with my grandpa is a cherished boyhood memory. He intuitively knew where the crappie, bluegill, and lake perch were hiding. As we neared one of those areas, Grandpa would turn off his outboard motor and let the boat float to the ideal spot. Then he would tell the person sitting at the front to quietly let down the anchor, and we'd all bait our hooks.

In time, my brothers and I learned the best ways to lure the fish toward the bait.

Our temptation to sin follows a similar process. James 1:14–15 informs us that the ultimate source of temptation is our own evil desire, lust, or craving. If we give in, it leads to sin and its consequences. This is true for everyone: "Each person is tempted when he is lured and enticed by his own desire." The process of temptation follows four steps.

We are "lured and enticed." Residing in our corrupt nature, lust drags us toward sin much like a fish is drawn from its hiding place. Powerful desires bait the hook, and too often we are not strong enough to resist. John Owen warns, "Do not flatter yourself that you can hold out. There are secret lusts that lie dormant, lurking in your hearts, temporarily quiet, waiting for the opportunity of temptation to befall you. They will then rise, argue, cry, disquiet, seduce, with perseverance, until either they are killed or satisfied."[1]

The devil is the instigator of the original temptation in the garden of Eden. But ever since Adam and Eve took the bait, we have all possessed a nature that swims toward sin (see Mark 7:21; Rom. 5:12).

Conception takes place. When our will surrenders to the temptation generated by our corrupt desires, we bite the hook. Evil is "conceived," and a pregnancy of sin begins. This sin grows and grows, longing for the day of its delivery.

Sin is born. Conception "gives birth to sin"—the numerous ways we fail to measure up to, or we transgress, God's law. There are sins of commission and omission, sins of disobedience and defiance, sins of action and attitude. All these sins and more originate in our thinking, desires, and will. Just as each fish responds best to its own custom-designed lure or carefully baited hook, so

---

1. John Owen, *Temptation: Resisted and Repulsed,* ed. Richard Rushing (Edinburgh: Banner of Truth Trust, 2007), 26.

our sinful desires seek their own personal fulfillment. The human heart is endlessly creative in the ways it expresses sin.

The offspring matures. Sin "when it is fully grown brings forth death." When temptation's goal is met and sin is born, a spiritual death occurs. However, physical death may also be implied here, since James addresses the possibility that some bodily sicknesses are caused by unrepentant sin (see 5:14–16). At minimum, however, sin is always at least injurious to our souls. Believers in Jesus no longer need to fear eternal separation from God. However, sin interrupts the sweetness of our fellowship with God, and so we should quickly repent and confess it to him (see 1 John 1:8–10).

The kinds of temptation we experience are limited only by the innovation of our corrupt hearts, which is considerable. The biblical record does not make an explicit connection between the cycle of temptation taught by James and the descent of King David into sin. However, David's surrender to sexual desire illustrates how the four-step process can work (see 2 Sam. 11:1–6). First, while his army was at war, the idle king was lured to the palace rooftop by his lust. Second, David's will surrendered to his desire to take Bathsheba for himself, and he conceived a plot to achieve his desire. Third, the sinful expression of his corrupt desire was born. (In this case, a literal baby was conceived!) Fourth, and finally, David's sin led to death when Bathsheba's husband and some other soldiers were killed, as well as the baby who was conceived in sin (see 2 Sam. 11:14–17; 12:15–17). David's relationship with God was interrupted as well. The cycle was complete.

TALK TO YOURSELF. Where have you seen the cycle of temptation and sin at work in your life? What are the most common ways your desires bait the hook?

TALK TO GOD. Psalm 51 is David's prayer of confession for his sin with Bathsheba. Make this prayer your own.

TALK TO OTHERS. Do you need help to overcome a specific temptation? Seek help from a pastor, mentor, or biblical counselor.

38. What Is the Devil's Part in Temptation?

Jesus, full of the Holy Spirit, returned from the Jordan and was led by the Spirit in the wilderness for forty days, being tempted by the devil. . . . And when the devil had ended every temptation, he departed from him until an opportune time.
(Luke 4:1–2, 13)

God is never the source of temptation to sin. Instead, the cycle begins with strong desires in our hearts. So perhaps you're wondering if the devil is involved at all. Yes, he is.

We learn much from Satan's tempting of Jesus. Though Jesus did not have a sin nature as we do, the devil struck at his humanity with full force, and yet Jesus endured. From the devil's attacks and Jesus's obedience despite them, we learn five ways Satan is involved in tempting us to sin. We also notice the chief means to resist the devil as our Savior did.

Satan attacks when you're most vulnerable. The devil's first temptation appealed to a legitimate physical need for food. Jesus "was hungry" after his forty-day fast (Luke 4:2). Like a shrewd hunter, Satan aimed his arrow at the bull's-eye of Jesus's vulnerability. Philip Ryken explains, "What Jesus suffered in the wilderness would have killed a weaker man. His condition was critical. At the end of forty days he was closer to death than at any other point in his life, except the crucifixion."[2] Be mindful of your weakness and watch out when you are most susceptible to Satan's attacks.

Satan casts doubt on God's Word. The devil planted a big "If" in the mind of the Savior: "If you are the Son of God" was a subtle attack on the integrity of God's words (4:3). God had just declared Jesus to be his Son at his baptism (see Matt. 3:17), but now the devil challenged that word. Satan hasn't changed. He's the same sneaky serpent who successfully used an identical tactic on Eve: "Did God actually say?" (Gen. 3:1). As he attempted with both Jesus and Eve, the devil plants the seed of doubt concerning Scripture.

Satan feeds fleshly pride. Jesus successfully resisted Satan's first attack, so the devil tempted him to break the first commandment by worshipping another god (see Ex. 20:3). Satan appealed to humanity's innate desire for position and power by showing Jesus all the kingdoms of the world and promising, "If you, then, will worship me, it will all be yours" (Luke 4:7). This was an attempt to get the Son of God to grab what rightfully belonged to him before it was time and without having to suffer. But this temptation was a lie! God's plan to exalt his Son throughout the world required the cross. No cross, no crown. No humiliation, no exaltation (see Phil. 2:8–11). When tempted to act in self-will, remember that you are making a choice of *who* to worship.

Satan encourages us to test God. In the third temptation, the devil tried to manipulate Jesus into foolishly misapplying Scripture by taking a five-hundred-foot "leap of faith." Satan took him to the pinnacle of the temple and said, "If you are the Son of God, throw yourself down from here, for it is written . . ." and then he quoted two Bible verses out of context (Luke 4:9–10; see also v. 11).

2. Philip Graham Ryken, *Luke*, Reformed Expository Commentary (Phillipsburg, NJ: P&R Publishing, 2009), 1:154.

109

But the living Word answered the devil by properly quoting from Deuteronomy, where we read of how Israel put God to the test by demanding that Moses produce water for them. If you are tempted to put God to the test, remind yourself of his many promises, as well as his commands to trust him instead.

Satan never gives up. When "the devil had ended every temptation, he departed from [Jesus] until an opportune time." The devil is relentless. Just as he hounded Jesus all the way to the cross, so he never tires of tempting you. He's always on the hunt, always waiting for an opportune time. You must "resist him, firm in your faith" (1 Peter 5:9), the same way Jesus did.

Three times, the devil tempted Jesus. Three times, Jesus answered, "It is written" (Luke 4:4, 8, 12). We can fight the deceiver's lies with "the sword of the Spirit, which is the word of God" (Eph. 6:17).

TALK TO YOURSELF. In the preface to *The Screwtape Letters,* C. S. Lewis writes, "There are two equal and opposite errors into which our race can fall about the devils. One is to disbelieve in their existence. The other is to believe, and to feel an excessive and unhealthy interest in them. They themselves are equally pleased by both errors."[3] As you reflect on your life with Christ up to now, do you see yourself drifting into either of these errors? Why?

TALK TO GOD. Do you ever act irresponsibly, contrary to biblical wisdom, and then expect God to protect you? If so, talk to God about it.

3. C. S. Lewis, *The Screwtape Letters with "Screwtape Proposes a Toast"* (New York: HarperCollins, 2013), ix.

TALK TO OTHERS. Talk to a pastor, mentor, or mature believer about the temptation that concerns you most and ask them to pray with you.

39. Dead to Sin and Alive to God

So you also must consider yourselves dead to sin and alive to God in Christ Jesus. (Rom. 6:11)

To comprehend the inner conflicts we face in our quest for godliness, we must do a helicopter flyover of Romans 6 and 7. Today, we'll hover over Romans 6, and tomorrow we'll survey Romans 7. In these chapters, the apostle Paul provides a glimpse into his own struggle against the power of indwelling sin and gives us Christ-centered hope.

Romans 6 presents the correct way to win the war against sin: through ongoing recognition that, by virtue of our spiritual union with Christ, we are already "dead to sin and alive to God." Since we know this is true, we must embrace it by faith; we "must consider" this truth. The word *consider* (or "reckon" in some translations) is an accounting term used by a bookkeeper who records an actual possession on one's account. Paul urges us to recognize (reckon) what is true of our spiritual condition before God in Christ. "We reckon ourselves dead to sin when we respond to temptation as a dead man would."[4]

---

4. William MacDonald, *Believer's Bible Commentary*, ed. Art Farstad (Nashville: Thomas Nelson, 1995), 1702.

One of my favorite musicals, *Fiddler on the Roof*, provides an illustration of this life-changing truth. The main character is a Jewish man living in Tsarist Russia who struggles to accept the cultural changes that are turning his world upside down, especially the non-arranged marriages of three of his daughters. Tradition—the glue that holds his ideal world together—begins to dissolve before his eyes. The oldest daughter is in love with the village tailor, but no one knows except the two of them, and the meddling village matchmaker has other plans in mind. The second daughter finds her affections drawn to a young, outspoken revolutionary and follows her arrested boyfriend to Siberia, where they are married.

The youngest daughter, however, breaks all molds by going further than her father can accept. At least her older sisters married fellow Jews, but she falls in love with a Gentile. She is treading on forbidden territory. When her father learns of the elopement, disillusionment floods his face, followed by a look of inner resolve. "She is dead to us," he says to his wife. According to the custom of his day, their daughter will not be spoken of or welcomed into their home. She is considered dead, and her father will consciously resist any memory of her.

In the same way, you must continually count, or reckon, this to be so: your old nature is dead since you "have died with Christ" (Rom. 6:8). You must reject the flesh. You must not welcome it into your heart's home. You must not let remaining sin "reign in your mortal body, to make you obey its passions" (v. 12). You must shun the presentation of "your members to sin as instruments for unrighteousness" but instead present yourself to God as one who has "been brought from death to life, and your members to God as instruments for righteousness" (v. 13). The old man must be dead to you!

Likewise, you must consider the second and equally valuable part of your new reality: you are "alive to God." The Holy Spirit regenerated your soul; he breathed new life into you and created in you repentant faith by the instrument of the gospel (see Rom. 10:14). You are now spiritually awakened and alive to God. He breathed new life into you and made you a partaker "of the divine nature, having escaped from the corruption that is in the world because of sinful desire" (2 Peter 1:4).

In Christ, we are dead to sin and alive to God. This is our reality. But to fight off temptation, we must appreciate this truth and constantly speak it to ourselves.

TALK TO YOURSELF. Embrace this reality in Christ: "But now that you have been set free from sin and have become slaves of God, the fruit you get leads to sanctification and its end, eternal life" (Rom. 6:22). Remind yourself of this!

TALK TO GOD. Write a prayer that expresses your understanding of being dead to sin and alive to God.

TALK TO OTHERS. Read through Romans 6 with another believer in Christ. Discuss the realities that are yours in Christ and some ways to apply them.

40. Victory in Jesus

Wretched man that I am! Who will deliver me from this body of death? Thanks be to God through Jesus Christ our Lord! (Rom. 7:24–25)

I have a love-hate relationship with dandelions. Though the bright yellow blossoms are attractive to the eye, I don't appreciate how they invade our lawn and go to seed almost overnight. To get rid of them, I've got only two options. I could pick off the blooms one by one, only to see them reappear, or I could kill the plants at the root. Obviously, one approach is more effective than the other. In a similar way, we may put all our effort into picking off the blooms of sin, only to see them reappear, or we can attack the root. Which approach is most likely to produce lasting change?

In Romans 7, the apostle exposes a common but faulty way we view holiness. We often think that by working from the outside in, by diligently keeping the law, we can eliminate sin. But Paul confronts this flawed view of sanctification by making it clear that the law cannot convert the soul, control sinful passions, or change the inner person. This does not mean the law is bad. On the contrary, God's law is good because it reveals his righteousness and exposes our sinfulness (see v. 7), but it is insufficient to deal with our root problem. That's why we need Jesus!

The gospel is "the law of liberty" (James 1:25). The good news about Jesus is the only truth that can set us free. Restrictions may teach us how to pick off the blooms of sin, but they cannot get to the root; they cannot change our hearts. That is the work of the Spirit. To illustrate this fundamental truth, Paul states three facts, offers proof of each, and then draws a conclusion.

The law is spiritual, but man is fleshly, "sold under sin" (Rom. 7:14). The flesh is the principle of sin that continues to express itself through our minds and bodies. As proof, Paul confesses that he still does what he doesn't want to do and fails to do what he wants to do and knows he should do (see vv. 15–16). Therefore, he concludes that indwelling sin is the root problem: "So now it is no longer I who do it, but sin that dwells within me" (v. 17).

Nothing "good dwells in [us], that is, in [our] flesh" (Rom. 7:18). We are totally depraved. Sin has spread to every part of our being. As proof, Paul expresses his desire to do good and his inability to do so perfectly. Instead, he says, "the evil I do not want is what I keep on doing" (v. 19). His conclusion is the same: sin that "dwells within" is the root problem (v. 20).

When we "want to do right, evil lies close at hand" (Rom. 7:21). The proof Paul offers is the perpetual war raging within him (see vv. 22–23). Once again, he concludes that sin is the root problem: "the law of sin that dwells in my members" (v. 23).

Repeatedly, Paul confronts the reality of our struggle to be holy, and each time his conclusion is the same: *indwelling sin is the root problem.* Thankfully, that is not the end of the story. Like the apostle, we may cry out, "Wretched man that I am! Who will deliver me from this body of death?" but our ultimate victory is already on its way. "Thanks be to God through Jesus Christ our Lord!" The root of sin, which works through the body and brings it to death, has been severed by the victory of Christ. Its influence remains within us, but God will eventually defeat it at the final resurrection. "The sting of death is sin, and the power of sin is the law. But thanks be to God, who gives us the victory through our Lord Jesus Christ" (1 Cor. 15:56–57).

TALK TO YOURSELF. Thomas Schreiner writes, "Conflict with sin continues even though the lordship of sin has been shattered."[5] How does knowing that sin's dominion is broken help you to confront your sin struggles?

TALK TO GOD. Write a prayer of thanksgiving for the ultimate victory over sin that Christ has achieved for you.

TALK TO OTHERS. Are you stuck in a pattern of sin and needing help to get to the root so that you can break free? Reach out to a pastor, mentor, or biblical counselor.

5. Thomas R. Schreiner, *Paul: Apostle of God's Glory in Christ* (Downers Grove, IL: InterVarsity Press, 2001), 258.

DRINKING FROM GOD'S FOUNTAIN OF FORGIVENESS

41. Look and Keep On Looking

*And as Moses lifted up the serpent in the wilderness, so
must the Son of Man be lifted up, that whoever believes in
him may have eternal life. (John 3:14–15)*

The book of Numbers records an unusual event that took place
during Israel's wandering in the wilderness. As God's people
journeyed, they became impatient and grumbled "against God
and against Moses" over their lack of water and preferred foods
(Num. 21:5). In response, "the LORD sent fiery serpents among
the people, and they bit the people, so that many people of Israel
died" (v. 6).

The Israelites immediately repented, confessed their sin to
Moses, and pleaded with him to intercede. "So Moses prayed for
the people" (Num. 21:7). God answered, "Make a fiery serpent and
set it on a pole, and everyone who is bitten, when he sees it, shall
live" (v. 8). Just a look—the simple look of faith—brought God's
healing. In this historical event, and Jesus's application of it to himself, we see three truths to embrace concerning God's forgiveness.

Forgiveness comes to those who realize the guilt of their sin. Before the sinning people could be forgiven, they had to admit, "We have sinned" (Num. 21:7). The snakebites brought them to the place of conviction. Only then were they ready to plead for forgiveness. One of the two guilty thieves hanging next to Jesus had a similar response. While one thief joined the crowd in launching accusations at the Savior, the other criminal realized his sinfulness. He knew he deserved to die, and so he turned the eyes of his heart to Jesus in faith (see Luke 23:39–42). As a result, he joined Jesus in paradise that very day.

Forgiveness comes to those who recognize their need for an intercessor. When the people realized the guilt of their sin, they immediately turned to Moses saying, "Pray to the LORD" (Num. 21:7). Every guilty sinner knows we cannot simply waltz into God's presence. We need a representative, an intercessor, a mediator. The sacrificial laws and rituals in the book of Leviticus repeatedly make this clear. Thankfully, God provided the one and only perfect priest to intercede for us: Jesus (see 1 Tim. 2:5–6; 1 John 1:8–2:1).

Forgiveness comes to those who look to God alone to provide the remedy. Only God could provide the healing that the people needed. By looking at the bronze serpent, they looked to God with eyes of faith (see Num. 21:8–9). Sadly, however, the bronze serpent eventually became an idol that later Israelites worshipped (see 2 Kings 18:4). True saving faith does not look to statues or human priests. It looks to God as the only one who can provide salvation and to Jesus as the only qualified priest. The Bible is clear that this faith in God alone is the only way for helpless sinners to be saved (see Rom. 5:6–10).

In the gospel of John, Jesus reveals that the bronze serpent was a symbol of himself: "As Moses lifted up the serpent in the wilderness, so must the Son of Man be lifted up." Jesus was making a comparison. As God provided the means by which snake-bitten people could be physically healed through faith, so he provided the only means by which our souls may find healing and restoration.

Like the snake-bitten Israelites, we are helpless to remedy our sin problem. But when we look to Jesus—the only one who can intercede for us—with eyes of faith, we are redeemed from slavery to sin, are fully forgiven, and receive the gift of eternal life. Having first looked to Jesus to save us from the penalty of our sin, we must keep on looking to him to guide us through the wilderness of sin and into our land of promise.

TALK TO YOURSELF. When you feel guilty about sin, do you tend to look inward or upward? Do you try to fix yourself, or do you look to Jesus? How might you encourage your gaze to go to the right place?

TALK TO GOD. Write a prayer that simply looks to Jesus as the remedy for your sin.

TALK TO OTHERS. Read Numbers 21:4–9 with a friend in Christ. Discuss its correlation to the death of Christ. Then read Luke 23:39–42 and discuss the "look of faith."

42. Cleaning Up the Pollution

Create in me a clean heart, O God, and renew a right spirit within me. (Ps. 51:10)

The Cuyahoga River Fire of 1969 is one of the most significant fires in history. On the morning of June 22, 1969, an oil slick on the river caught fire. Though it burned for only half an hour, the blaze caught the attention of the nation. The following year, *Time* magazine featured the fire in its cover article, which sparked ecological conversation that resulted in the founding of the Environmental Protection Agency.

Another article employs vivid language to describe the condition of the river at that time: "The water was nearly always covered in oil slicks, and it bubbled like a deadly stew. Sometimes rats floated by, their corpses so bloated they were practically the size of dogs."[1] The author of the article says this was "disturbing,"—yet much more disturbing than environmental contamination is the pollution that sin brings to our hearts.

In Psalm 51, we hear the expression of a deeply troubled conscience. Here, as King David comes to grips with his sin and its toxic consequences, he begs God for a deep cleaning. In his excellent book on the dynamics of the human heart, Craig Troxel explains that this psalm "addresses the pollution of iniquity as David seeks forgiveness for his adultery with Bathsheba. One striking feature of the psalm is how much David speaks in terms of his need to be washed clean. He feels the pollution of his sin."[2]

1. Lorraine Boissoneault, "The Cuyahoga River Caught Fire at Least a Dozen Times, but No One Cared until 1969," *Smithsonian*, June 19, 2019, https://www.smithsonianmag.com/history/cuyahoga-river-caught-fire-least-dozen-times-no-one-cared-until-1969-180972444/.
2. A. Craig Troxel, *With All Your Heart: Orienting Your Mind, Desires, and Will toward Christ* (Wheaton, IL: Crossway, 2020), 84.

- "Blot out my transgressions" (v. 1)
- "Wash me thoroughly from my iniquity" (v. 2)
- "Cleanse me from my sin" (v. 2)
- "Purge me with hyssop, and I shall be clean" (v. 7)
- "Wash me, and I shall be whiter than snow" (v. 7)

King David truly felt polluted, as he should have. He had misused his authority, stolen another man's wife, and committed murder. She was pregnant with his son out of wedlock. Her husband was dead, and the blood was on his hands—and the entire kingdom knew it (see 2 Sam. 11). His sin was "ever before" him (Ps. 51:3), and feelings of regret and uncleanness had the potential to haunt him forever. But did it have to be this way? Or was there a way for his heart to be fully cleansed? Thankfully, yes. David turned to the One who can clean the most polluted heart.

It's worth noting that David's repeated plea for cleansing is rooted in his awareness of God's gracious character: "Have mercy on me, O God, according to your steadfast love; according to your abundant mercy blot out my transgressions" (Ps. 51:1). David's plea was based on God's "abundant mercy," not any sense of the entitlement he may have felt when he sinned. The pollution of sin casts a dark shadow over our souls, which dampens our joy. Therefore, having received the cleansing that God promises to the repentant sinner, David sings, "Restore to me the joy of your salvation" (v. 12).

The Cuyahoga River fire took place more than fifty years ago, but some toxicity remains in its waters to this day. Some doubt that the river will ever be fully clean. Perhaps you doubt that you can ever be fully clean as well. Though the toxicity of sin remains in our hearts, God's cleansing of our sin-pollution is infinitely more thorough than any environmental cleanup.

TALK TO YOURSELF. Consider this thought from Craig Troxel: "Iniquity not only condemns us and makes us feel guilty, it pollutes us and makes us feel dirty."[3] How have you felt the dirtiness of sin, either of your sins or of sins committed against you?

TALK TO GOD. Pray through Psalm 51. Be honest before God about the ways you feel polluted. Ask him to wash you thoroughly. Ask him to help you to believe his promise to cleanse you. Ask him to restore to you the joy of your salvation.

TALK TO OTHERS. In Psalm 51:13, David determines to use his experience of the cleansing grace of God to teach others the way of repentance and restoration: "Then I will teach transgressors your ways, and sinners will return to you." Is there someone in your church or family who is overcome by the pollution of their sin? Reach out to them. Be a hope dispenser by telling them your story of God's triumphant grace.

43. The Immeasurable Joy of Being Forgiven

How blessed is he whose wrongdoing is forgiven, whose sin is covered! How blessed is a person whose guilt the LORD does not take into account, and in whose spirit there is no deceit!
(Ps. 32:1–2 NASB)

What greater joy can there be than to know that our sins are forgiven, to know with certainty that the guilt of every sin we've ever

3. Troxel, 85.

committed has been removed, to know that we stand before the Lord fully accepted, fully clothed in his righteousness, and never to be condemned? Surely there's nothing that thrills the soul quite like the fullness of God's forgiveness!

Today's verses are an outburst of praise to God from someone who has experienced cleansing in an enormous way. In the opening words of Psalm 32, King David remembers vividly what it means to confess his sin and then to know his "wrongdoing is forgiven." He recalls what it feels like to have the crushing weight of guilt removed from his troubled soul. And from this wellspring of joy, he brings both comfort and counsel.

Be comforted to know that your "sin is covered" and "the LORD does not take into account" your guilt any longer. Both phrases emphasize that when God forgives sin, he releases the debt so completely that there is no longer any record of it.

The Old Testament phrase *sin is covered* means that God hides sin when he sees an acceptable sacrifice in its place. God slew an animal and provided "garments of skins" to clothe Adam and Eve (Gen. 3:21). In like manner, God crushed his only begotten Son in your place, putting "him to grief" as Jesus willingly became "an offering for guilt" (Isa. 53:10).

To "not take into account" means that God no longer holds guilty any sinner who displays repentant faith. In their spirit "there is no deceit," for they have honestly faced their sin. When you own up to your wrongdoings before God, he "blots out your transgressions" and "will not remember your sins" against you (Isa. 43:25).

Be counseled by the dire consequences of David's initial refusal to admit his sin. Psalm 32:3–4 describes David's self-imposed pain. When he "kept silent" about his sin, his "bones wasted away" as his guilt-laden conscience groaned "all day long" (v. 3). "Day and night," God's chastening "hand was heavy" on him (v. 4). His "strength was dried up" just as when "the heat of summer" saps a body of its energy (v. 4). Unconfessed sin always diminishes our physical health. Since God created us as embodied souls, our spiritual state always impacts our physical, and vice versa.[4] Thankfully, David's experience doesn't end there.

As stubbornness robbed him of intimate fellowship with God, so David's decision to turn from pride and put on humility by submitting to God's discipline restored his joy. David knew what he had lost—sweet communion with God—and he wanted it back. "I acknowledged my sin to you," he prays, and "did not cover my iniquity; I said, 'I will confess my transgressions to the LORD,' and you forgave the iniquity of my sin" (Ps. 32:5).

When our consciences are tormented by the guilt of our sin, we too may humbly confess to God and experience the immeasurable joy of forgiveness.

TALK TO YOURSELF. Read Proverbs 28:13. Can you think of a time when you experienced this truth in your life?

TALK TO GOD. Write a prayer of confession to God. Be specific. Ask him to cleanse you. Thank him for the removal of your guilt because of the once-for-all, fully accepted sacrifice of the Lord Jesus Christ.

TALK TO OTHERS. Read Psalm 103 with a friend in Jesus. Discuss the many divine blessings that those who belong to the Lord possess. List them in your journal.

---

4. For a fuller explanation of this dynamic, see my thirty-one-day devotional, *Anxiety: Knowing God's Peace* (Phillipsburg, NJ: P&R Publishing, 2019).

44. More Counsel from a Stubborn King

I will instruct you and teach you in the way you should go;
I will counsel you with my eye upon you. Be not like a horse
or a mule, without understanding. (Ps. 32:8–9)

To be counseled by someone who humbly admits they have "been there, done that" is more helpful than to receive pious platitudes from one who stands aloof. We saw this in the previous reading when we witnessed King David's turn from prideful stubbornness to humble confession. Afterward, he felt a newfound appreciation for the breadth and depth of God's forgiveness. Today, we benefit from David's counsel again.

David's agonizing impenitence seared him with a longing to urge others to learn from his failure. He warns us against stubbornly refusing to admit our sin. In Psalm 32:6–11, he prays to God before transitioning to giving counsel. David asks God to move in the hearts of godly men and women so that we will "offer prayer to [God] at a time when [he] may be found" (v. 6). In other words, David's concern is that we do not procrastinate as he did. Therefore, he pleads with God to work quickly in our hearts. The once-stubborn, now-humbled king has experienced God as his "hiding place" who preserves him "from trouble" and surrounds him "with shouts of deliverance" (v. 7). David expresses his burden: "I will instruct you and teach you in the way you should go." Three directives emerge from the repentant king's counsel.

Seek the Lord immediately. Don't wait until God's discipline forces you to confess your sin. Don't be "like a horse or a mule, without understanding, which must be curbed with bit and bridle" (Ps. 32:9). Ignoring the conviction of the Holy Spirit leads to hard-heartedness, which in turn may eventually result in the Lord's ears being closed to your prayers (see Prov. 28:9). Don't put off confession because you know God is gracious. That is a presumptuous sin (see Ps. 19:13).

Trust in the Lord's loving-kindness. "Many are the sorrows of the wicked, but steadfast love surrounds the one who trusts in the LORD" (Ps. 32:10). When pride spurs you to dig in your heels and refuse to repent, you're acting like an unbeliever rather than one who loves the Lord. Remember, the way to God is thrown open to you in Christ. Trust God to be "faithful and just to forgive" you when you confess your sins (1 John 1:9). By agreeing with God concerning the guilt of your sin (which is what it means to *confess*), you also declare that you trust him to cleanse you from all your sin through the blood of Christ.

Rejoice in God's righteousness. David's last piece of counsel from Psalm 32 is this: "Be glad in the LORD, and rejoice, O righteous, and shout for joy, all you upright in heart!" (v. 11). An upright heart belongs to the person who has been cleansed by God. When you confess your sin to God and receive his gracious forgiveness, your logical response should be to shout for joy.

We do not find joy by pretending that we have no sin. Psalm 32 makes that clear. However, when we repent and humbly turn to the Savior in faith, we will "rejoice with joy that is inexpressible and filled with glory" (1 Peter 1:8).

TALK TO YOURSELF. Read Proverbs 1:24–33. These verses personify godly wisdom as a woman who calls us to listen to her and follow her counsel. Think about a time in your life when you refused to listen and perhaps suffered some of the consequences described in this passage.

TALK TO GOD. In your journal, write out another prayer of confession to God. Be specific. Dig deeper than your actions to the stubbornness or other heart issues that lie underneath them. Confess these to God as well.

TALK TO OTHERS. Is there someone you know who would benefit if you shared your "forgiveness story" with them, just as David did with us?

45. Love Grows in the Soil of Forgiveness

You did not anoint my head with oil, but she has anointed my feet with ointment. Therefore I tell you, her sins, which are many, are forgiven—for she loved much. But he who is forgiven little, loves little. (Luke 7:46–47)

Let all bitterness and wrath and anger and clamor and slander be put away from you, along with all malice. Be kind to one another, tenderhearted, forgiving one another, as God in Christ forgave you. (Eph. 4:31–32)

Forgiveness from God produces fruits of sanctification—especially love for God and others—when it is intentionally remembered. A Christian who does not love God or others and refuses to forgive is an inconceivable contradiction. At best, resentment and its offspring, bitterness, reveal that such a person's faith is immature and shortsighted. At worst, lack of obedience to God and love for others exposes the fatal state of a heart that has not been effectually touched by grace. Consider the descriptions of God's forgiveness that we have been thinking about in the past four readings. These are critical points of application to draw from them.

In the first of today's Scripture passages, Jesus teaches that a person's love for God is evidence that God has forgiven them. As you remember the depth of the forgiveness you've received through faith in Jesus, your heart is stirred to love him more deeply. Like the woman who washed Jesus's feet with her tears, if you regularly ponder the depth of your sinfulness, you will appreciate the breadth of God's forgiveness and grow in humility and love for him.

But the opposite is true as well. If you forget God's forgiveness of your sins, you will become proud and calloused. You who have been forgiven much will begin to act like those who think they have been forgiven little. You'll become slow to forgive others. When you fall short of displaying gracious, Christlike forgiveness, the soil of your heart is in danger of cultivating a form of unbelief the Bible calls the "root of bitterness" that "springs up and causes trouble" (Heb. 12:15). Fight against this by remembering how much you have been forgiven. Such a practice cultivates love and tenderheartedness.

Therefore, our second Scripture passage for today directs you to practice biblical love by forgiving others. You are commanded to "put away" bitterness and all its cousins and to put on the kindness of God. This leads to forgiving others just "as God in Christ forgave you." The context of this command is the larger directive to "put off your old self . . . to be renewed in the spirit of your minds, and to put on the new self" (Eph. 4:22–24). In other words, knowing who you are in Christ should propel your heart toward, not away from, the people who hurt you.

Jesus also maintained this important connection. In the prayer pattern that he gave his disciples, he instructs us, "Pray then like this. . . . 'Forgive us our debts, as we also have forgiven our debtors'" (Matt. 6:9, 12). Jesus then gives a promise and a warning: "If you forgive others their trespasses, your heavenly Father will also forgive you, but if you do not forgive others their trespasses, neither will your Father forgive your trespasses" (vv. 14–15). Daily awareness of our own sinfulness will lead us to frequently ask God for his forgiveness, which will keep our hearts sensitive and forgiving toward those who wrong us.

TALK TO YOURSELF. Read Ephesians 4:17–32. Is there a specific area of your life that the Holy Spirit is directing you to address? What sinful attitudes or actions do you need to put off? What evidence of Christlike love do you need to put on? List them in your journal.

TALK TO GOD. In your journal, write out a prayer of thanksgiving for the depth of God's forgiveness of your sins, and ask him to soften the soil of your heart so that you are quick to forgive others.

TALK TO OTHERS. David Powlison writes, "The gospel embodies peace-making power."[5] Remembering the work of Christ on your behalf should move you to reconcile with other believers when you have conflicts. Is there someone in your church, your family, your workplace, or elsewhere who has wronged you but whom you refuse to forgive? Ask a mature Christian to help you to take steps toward forgiveness and reconciliation.

---

5. David Powlison, *Safe and Sound: Standing Firm in Spiritual Battles* (Greensboro, NC: New Growth Press, 2019), 29.

REPLACING AFFECTIONS

46. Realign Your Heart's Affections

Incline my heart to your testimonies, and not to selfish gain!
... Your testimonies are my heritage forever, for they are the
joy of my heart. I incline my heart to perform your statutes
forever, to the end. (Ps. 119:36, 111–12)

Thomas Chalmers, a Scottish mathematician, political economist, and leader of the Free Church of Scotland in the early 1800s, drew attention to the necessity of transformed desires in his best-known sermon, "The Expulsive Power of a New Affection." In it, Chalmers argues that true godliness cannot be gained simply by withdrawing from worldly desires. Rather, our natural affections must be replaced by a new, supernatural affection for God that is birthed by the Holy Spirit through the gospel. He wrote, "Such is the grasping tendency of the human heart that it must have a something to lay hold of—and which, if wrested away without the substitution of another something in its place, would leave a void and a vacancy as painful to the mind as hunger is to the natural system."[1] This premise is not

---

1. Thomas Chalmers, *The Expulsive Power of a New Affection* (repr., Wheaton, IL: Crossway, 2020), 36. This sermon is also available for free online—for example, at www.monergism.com.

the novel idea of a theologian from bygone days but is thoroughly biblical, as we will see in the next few readings.

Today's verses reveal both our need for God to change our inner affections and our personal responsibility to realign our hearts to the priorities of his Word. At the moment of our conversion, God worked a fundamental change in the nature and posture of our hearts. We thought about that in reading 32. But when it comes to progressive sanctification, we must play an active role in our hearts' ongoing realignment.

The psalmist pleads with God, "Incline my heart to your testimonies." In doing so, he admits his inability to accomplish the transforming work that is needed at the deepest level of his heart. To *incline* means to turn or bend. He wanted his heart to be bent no longer toward "selfish gain" but instead toward God's "testimonies." Like the psalmist, you need to be aware of your natural bents and plead with God to *bend your heart* in a different direction.

However, the psalmist understands that he needs to do more than pray. Alongside prayer, he embraces his obligation to find joy in the Word not merely as an academic but as a disciple whose aim is to become more obedient each day. Finding Scripture to be his heart's joy, he prays, "I incline my heart to perform your statutes forever, to the end." Notice that he doesn't merely say, "God, change my heart." He also chooses to delight in the Word in order to shift his heart's affections. Like the psalmist, you need to cultivate the habit of communing with God by meditating on his Word. As time goes on, this shifts your affections away from self and toward the Lord.

God designed you and me to be driven by desire. The remedy for corrupt desires is not to stop desiring—that's impossible. We can't stop wanting any more than we can stop breathing. Instead, we need the purifying power of new affections. When we bend our hearts toward the Word of God, we will experience the gradual bending of our affections toward the God of the Word.

TALK TO YOURSELF. Thomas Chalmers writes, "The best way of casting out an impure affection is to admit a pure one, and, by the love of what is good, to expel the love of what is evil."[2] Why is this replacement principle so significant to growth in Christ?

TALK TO GOD. Think about one of your sin struggles. When you choose to sin, what do you think you are loving—at that moment—more than God? Like the psalmist, pray something like the following: "Incline my heart, O Lord, to your Word. Cause your testimonies to be the supreme joy of my heart, so that I may grow in obedience to your Word."

TALK TO OTHERS. Ask another believer or two to read the sermon "The Expulsive Power of a New Affection" with you and discuss how it affects your understanding of sanctification.

2. Chalmers, 65.

47. Reorder Your Desires

As obedient children, do not be conformed to the passions of your former ignorance. (1 Peter 1:14)

What causes quarrels and what causes fights among you? Is it not this, that your passions are at war within you? (James 4:1)

We do what we do because we want what we want, and we want what we want because we love what we love. Therefore, authentic transformation into Christlikeness begins at the level of our deepest desires: our loves.

In contrast, when we change our behavior without reorienting our affections toward God, we'll practice powerless moralism at best and prideful Pharisaism at worst. Jesus warns of this: "Woe to you, scribes and Pharisees, hypocrites! For you clean the outside of the cup and the plate, but inside they are full of greed and self-indulgence" (Matt. 23:25). Lasting change takes place by the power of the Holy Spirit as we immerse ourselves in the Word of God, which in turn engenders new affections. However, obstacles remain in our way.

Deep within our hearts are the "passions of [our] former ignorance," as Peter says in the first of today's verses. He urges us no longer to be driven by fleshly desires but to live like "obedient children" of God. Since the war against sin is a daily, moment-by-moment reality, we need to deny ourselves, take up our crosses daily, and follow Jesus (see Luke 9:23). As we learned in the last reading, this begins at the level of our passions.

Now, to be clear, not all desires are sinful. Craig Troxel explains this well: "God created us to desire. It is when we twist our desires toward inappropriate ends or in disproportionate levels that things go wrong. . . . Desire becomes sinful when it becomes excessive, even if the object of desire is lawful—like your work or honoring your parents or even loving your country."[3] Good desires go bad when they become ultimate: *any* desire that we put before God is an idol.

In the second verse for today, James exposes the self-centeredness of our desires when he explains that the "passions . . . at war" *within* us are the cause of conflicts *among* us. His first readers were Jewish followers of Christ who had been dispersed abroad by persecution. Even as James wrote to comfort and encourage them, he counseled them (and us) to repent of hedonistic cravings that often reveal themselves in conflicts. Residing in your heart are self-loving desires that are so determined to be satisfied that, when thwarted, they lead to conflicts with those who get in the way of their fulfillment. "You desire and do not have, so you murder. You covet and cannot obtain, so you fight and quarrel" (4:2).

Our natural tendency is to try to fulfill our desires independently of God. Even good desires become evil when we satisfy them ourselves in a fleshly manner: "You do not have, because you do not ask. You ask and do not receive, because you ask wrongly, to spend it on your passions" (4:2–3). When our interests are divided, we commit spiritual adultery against Christ, our Bridegroom (see v. 4).

Since we were created to worship and serve God alone, part of being remade in Christ involves constantly striving to keep Christ as the sole object of our worship and devotion.

TALK TO YOURSELF. The apostle John ends his first letter to those who have been born of God with the following warning:

3. A. Craig Troxel, *With All Your Heart: Orienting Your Mind, Desires, and Will toward Christ* (Wheaton, IL: Crossway, 2020), 73–75.

"Little children, keep yourselves from idols" (1 John 5:21). Do you recognize anyone or anything in your life that you have made ultimate—that is, more important than loving God? Consider memorizing 2 Corinthians 5:9.

TALK TO GOD. Confess your sinful thoughts and actions—and the disorderly desires that drive them.

TALK TO OTHERS. Talk to a pastor, an elder, a ministry leader, or a trusted friend whom you believe will be honest with you. Ask them if they see anything in your life, other than the Lord, that you have made the best or only thing.

48. Holy Habits

As he who called you is holy, you also be holy in all your conduct, since it is written, "You shall be holy, for I am holy."
(1 Peter 1:15–16)

Bad habits are easy to form but hard to break. You and I know this from personal experience.

The opposite is true of godly habits. Still, we are called to discipline ourselves for godliness through the power of the indwelling Spirit of God, who is committed to reshaping us into the image of Christ. This process includes replacing ungodly patterns with godly ones.

In 1 Peter 1:15–16, the apostle roots his call for us to transform our habits in a specific appeal for us to be like the One who saves us: "As he who called you is holy, you also be holy in all your conduct." Then Peter quotes from Leviticus 11:44, "You shall be holy, for I am holy"—God's command to Israel to reflect his holiness by being distinct from other nations.

God's holiness is his set-apartness. Kent Hughes is spot-on when he writes, "Holiness is essential to God's nature; it is not so much an attribute of God as it is the very foundation of his being. Holiness denotes the separateness or otherness of God."[4] Holiness distinguishes God from everything he created. "There is none like me in all the earth," God says (Ex. 9:14).

In part 1 of this book, we learned that the Greek word for saints—believers who are set apart by God for himself—means "holy ones." We saw that your current occupation is to become an obedient child since God called you with "a holy calling" (2 Tim. 1:9). To be holy is to live in such a way that you accurately reflect God to others. This does not mean being different for difference's sake or drawing attention to yourself through your outward appearance. But it means becoming like the Savior in character and attitude. This sober (not somber) approach to the Christian life is the believer's expected response to God's gracious salvation.

In Christ, we've been saved from lives of sin and destruction by the grace of God. Consequently, our present calling is to allow that same grace to empower us to reflect the Lord. We must pursue the complete transformation of life that proceeds from reorienting our inner desires, renewing our minds, and replacing sinful habits with righteous actions. Richard Baxter writes, "Till the sin be hated and the contrary grace or duty in practice, you have not at all overcome."[5] In other words, hating sin is not the same as

---

4. R. Kent Hughes, *Set Apart: Calling a Worldly Church to a Godly Life* (Wheaton, IL: Crossway Books, 2003), 18.

5. Richard Baxter, *A Christian Directory*, reprinted in *The Practical Works of the Rev. Richard Baxter* (London, 1830), 2:308, quoted in Dale W. Smith, ed., *Ore from the Puritans' Mine: Calling a Worldly Church to a Godly Life* (Grand Rapids: Reformation Heritage Books, 2020), 563.

overcoming it. In addition to changing our attitude about our sins, we must work to put godly disciplines in their place. Since we now belong to Christ, we must become more and more like him.

TALK TO YOURSELF. In his commentary on the book of Romans, Alva J. McClain wrote, "A Christian whose life is not what it ought to be often gives this excuse: 'I don't pretend to be a saint!' It doesn't matter what you pretend to be—if you are a Christian, *you are a saint!* . . . God never goes to a sinner and tells him to try to attain to sainthood. He picks us out of the mud, and He says, 'You are a saint.' We are not making believe. We are holy and must live in accordance with our position."[6] In what ways do you excuse any lack of progress in godliness?

TALK TO GOD. If you are guilty of excusing away any sin(s) in your life, talk to the Lord about it. Confess your sins and your excuses. Ask him to move your will to want to grow in holiness more than you naturally want to sin.

TALK TO OTHERS. Some habits are too hard to break on our own. If you feel defeated because of repeated failures, reach out to a mature believer and ask them to come alongside you.

6. Alva J. McClain, *Romans: The Gospel of God's Grace*, ed. Herman A. Hoyt (1973; repr., Winona Lake, IN: BMH Books, 1989), 43–44. Italics his.

49. Both/And

So put away all malice and all deceit and hypocrisy and envy and all slander. Like newborn infants, long for the pure spiritual milk, that by it you may grow up into salvation—if indeed you have tasted that the Lord is good. (1 Peter 2:1–3)

Holiness is not an either/or proposition; it's both/and. For the past few readings, we've been reminding ourselves of this key principle of Christian fruitfulness. It's not *either* put off sin *or* put on righteousness. It's both at the same time. The Holy Spirit is not simply set *against* the ungodly desires, attitudes, and actions that we should avoid, he's also committed to increasing our hunger for the ones we should *embrace*.

In today's Scripture passage, the apostle Peter presses us to "put away" specific sins, though his list is not exhaustive. This is expected since, in the last reading, we heard God's call to become holy as he is holy (1 Peter 1:15–16). It only makes sense, then, that Peter would name at least some forms of ungodliness that we should put to death.

What is unexpected, however, is what Peter tells us to pursue, which is more interaction with the sanctifying Word. Like a nursing baby, Peter says, you need to "long for the pure spiritual milk." You need an insatiable appetite for the pure, uncontaminated Word of God. A small appetite for the Scriptures will limit your growth, while a strong appetite will help you to flourish. A steady diet of the Word of God should be enjoyed in at least two venues.

Personal intake requires daily meditation and study, which is a key to your growth "into salvation." This is not referring to growth that leads *to* salvation but to the growth that should spring *out of* the salvation you have already received. In other words, if you have experienced conversion to Christ (as Peter says, "tasted that the Lord is good"), then you should crave the Word that feeds your faith. This instruction is consistent with what Peter learned from Jesus, who made it clear that feeding on "every word that comes from the mouth of God" is a necessity of life (Matt. 4:4).

Public intake of Scripture is also indispensable. Placing a high priority on listening to the public reading and preaching of the Word is nonnegotiable. In the last days, Paul warns, "people will be lovers of self" (2 Tim. 3:2) and, as a result, some professing Christians will turn their ears away from sound teaching and instead want to be tickled only with man-centered theories that make them feel good (see 2 Tim. 4:1–4). In contrast, faithful Christians keep participation in public worship—which includes listening to sound preaching—a high priority for themselves and their families. Do not forsake the community of your local church "as is the habit of some" (Heb. 10:25). Instead, delight to gather for worship and instruction so that you may grow in Christ, encourage other believers to keep pressing on, and be equipped for service.

The *put off / put on* discipline of the Christian life is essential to sanctification. However, if you begin at the level of your behavior, you are attempting to change yourself from the outside in. This will leave you frustrated by short-term success: you will be encouraged only for as long as your willpower lasts. Instead, you must learn to discern your heart's desires—your affections and longings—and implore God to change your heart through the instrument of his Word.

TALK TO YOURSELF. Read James 1:21. Sin must be put off and replaced by the sanctifying Word. What changes do you need to make concerning your intake of the Word, both personally and publicly?

TALK TO GOD. Is there a sin that the Holy Spirit has been pressing you to turn from?

TALK TO OTHERS. If you are not sure how to make changes to your Bible-intake habits, or need help to form them, find a mature Christian who can teach and mentor you.

50. Submit to the Divine Surgeon

They are not of the world, just as I am not of the world. Sanctify them in the truth; your word is truth. (John 17:16–17)

For the word of God is living and active, sharper than any two-edged sword, piercing to the division of soul and of spirit, of joints and of marrow, and discerning the thoughts and intentions of the heart. (Heb. 4:12)

The Bible is the only living book on the planet. As such, it breathes life into our souls and actively performs surgery on our inner person. Believers in Jesus have another marvel to consider: the Author of Scripture lives within us! Jesus promised us "the Spirit of truth, whom the world cannot receive, because it neither sees him nor knows him. You know him, for he dwells with you and will be in you" (John 14:17). In Christ, we are no longer "of the world" but are born anew by the Holy Spirit who changes us in response to Jesus's prayer: "Sanctify them in the truth; your word is truth." No man-made philosophy, behavioristic strategy, or self-help method contains such power! Only the Word of the living God can transform us from the inside out.

Hebrews 4:12 begins with the little word *for*. This connects back to the previous verses, in which we learn that Jesus, the Living Word, is our spiritual rest. When we place our faith in his finished work, we enter our Sabbath. We rest from the false belief that human works could ever be the basis of our acceptance by God (see Rom. 4:4–5). However, like God's people in the days of Moses and Joshua, we must guard our hearts from unbelief. We do this by striving "to enter that rest, so that no one may fall by the same sort of disobedience" (Heb. 4:11). Every exposure to the Word leaves us more accountable to God, and therefore Hebrews 4:12 compels us to stay in God's Word for five reasons.

The Bible is divine. From its first words, Scripture reveals God as the one who speaks life. Scripture is the record of what God thinks and what he has decided is essential for you to know. It is "the word of God." The Bible is the mind of God in written form and, as such, should have full authority over your mind.

The Bible can change your heart because it is alive. The word *living* could be translated "constantly actively alive." It is the recorded voice of Jesus Christ the Living Word, and, as such, it never rests. The more you fill your mind with its truth and submit your will to its authority, the more it is at work within you.

The Bible is "active." It energizes your spirit to make you productive, leading to an increased harvest of spiritual fruit. When the Word washes over your heart like a good rain nourishes the earth, God promises, "It shall not return to me empty, but it shall accomplish that which I purpose, and shall succeed in the thing for which I sent it" (Isa. 55:11). Time spent in your Bible is never wasted.

The Bible is a piercing book. The adjective *sharper* originates from the primitive root meaning "to cut." Scripture has cutting power; it penetrates. As the scalpel in the divine surgeon's hand, the Word cuts through to your innermost being. It heals as it wounds. It exposes cancer of the soul so that it may apply God's remedy.

The Bible helps you to discern "the thoughts and intentions of the heart." As you read, hear, and listen to the Word, the Spirit evaluates the deepest parts of your inner being, enabling you to see sins and blind spots. This moves you to repent of not only your outward behavior but also your loves.

Scripture is God's sanctifying agent. The Spirit employs it to purify the Son's bride for the day when she is finally presented to him. We need to humbly submit to the Divine Surgeon's good work.

TALK TO YOURSELF. Before you read your Bible, do you ask the Spirit to expose your heart?

TALK TO GOD. Open your Bible and pray through Psalm 139:23–24.

TALK TO OTHERS. Ask one or more fellow believers to share with you what they have recently learned from their study of the Bible.

RENEWING THE MIND

51. Godliness Requires Discipline

For this very reason, make every effort to supplement your
faith with virtue, and virtue with knowledge, and knowledge
with self-control, and self-control with steadfastness, and
steadfastness with godliness, and godliness with brotherly
affection, and brotherly affection with love. (2 Peter 1:5–7)

Thomas Alva Edison is arguably the greatest inventor of all time. Born into a businessman's family in 1847, he received little formal education. His mother guided the learning of her mischievous young boy, who loved to pull pranks and play practical jokes. Above all, though, he loved to read science books.

At the age of twelve, Edison started his first business: selling newspapers, candy, and sandwiches on passenger trains. Business grew to the point that he hired others to sell for him and, at the age of fifteen, published his own newspaper. One day, after Edison rescued a telegraph operator's son from the path of a railroad car, the man rewarded him with telegraph lessons. These came in handy when he developed hearing problems in his teens and needed to master the art of receiving news by telegraph for his own communication.

Edison would go on to obtain 1,093 United States patents, the most given to any individual, as he invented one creation after another. In one word, the reason for Edison's remarkable achievement is *discipline*. After all, he is often quoted as saying, "Genius is 1 percent inspiration and 99 percent perspiration." The same is true when it comes to godliness. Discipline is essential.

In today's verses, the apostle Peter says you must "make every effort to supplement" your faith with gradual growth. The word *supplement* does not mean that you *add* anything to faith to receive salvation but that your faith should be lavishly adorned by godly character qualities such as those mentioned above. Earlier in this book, we saw that we receive our justification before God solely by coming to him in empty-handed faith. Nevertheless, saving faith is alive; faith works to make us holy. John the Baptizer's preaching made this clear from the start: "Bear fruit in keeping with repentance" (Matt. 3:8).

The fruit we bear, however, is not the outcome of perspiration alone but is produced by grace. Peter assures us that God's power "has granted to us all things that pertain to life and godliness" (2 Peter 1:3). In Christ, you have all you need to be transformed into his likeness. You've become a partaker of "the divine nature" and, by God's gracious rescue, have "escaped from the corruption that is in the world because of sinful desire" (v. 4). When you were converted, the Spirit of Jesus forever changed the moral trajectory of your life. Now you must discipline yourself to walk that path.

In *Knowing Sin*, Mark Jones writes, "Indwelling sin is always ready to pounce. It is not lazy, though it breeds laziness."[1] We are prone to look for the easy way out, and spiritual growth and victory sometimes evade us. Our unredeemed flesh is attracted to

---

1. Mark Jones, *Knowing Sin: Seeing a Neglected Doctrine through the Eyes of the Puritans* (Chicago: Moody Publishers, 2022), 66.

simple formulas for instant godliness such as "Let go and let God" or "Just let Jesus take control." Slogans fail because they promise victory apart from the daily grind of discipline. That will never happen. Therefore, we need to change the way we think about spiritual growth.

TALK TO YOURSELF. In his classic little book *Thoughts for Young Men,* J. C. Ryle warns, "It is flying in the face of God's purposes to do as many do—to make the soul a servant of the body, and not the body a servant to the soul."[2] In what ways do you need to make your body your servant instead of your master?

TALK TO GOD. One of the ways the fruit of the Spirit becomes evident in our lives is through self-discipline. Why not stop and pray right now? Perhaps vocalize something like this: "Spirit of God, who lives within and empowers me to become like Christ, please develop self-discipline where it is lacking in me."

TALK TO OTHERS. Scripture repeatedly links our progress in godliness to self-discipline. Instead of passive slogans and surefire formulas, the Bible uses words like *discipline, strive, work out, train, flee,* and *pursue* (Luke 13:24; Phil. 2:12; 1 Tim. 4:7; 2 Tim. 2:22) There are simply no shortcuts to spiritual maturity. Ask a friend or mentor how they have grown in self-discipline and how it has helped their spiritual life.

2. John Charles Ryle, *Thoughts for Young Men* (1886; repr., Moscow, ID: Charles Nolan Publishers, 2002), 37.

52. Stay Awake

Therefore, preparing your minds for action, and being sober-minded, set your hope fully on the grace that will be brought to you at the revelation of Jesus Christ. (1 Peter 1:13)

Staying awake can be difficult for me, especially after a hard day's work. A nap in my recliner is an appealing and well-earned treat. But if I'm not careful, I may sleep too long and awake disoriented and sluggish. The same goes for our spiritual lives. When we get tired of fighting against the world, the flesh, and the devil, we may each be tempted to get comfortable in our spiritual recliner, kick up the footrest, and fall asleep. Instead, we must stay awake.

We find strength to fight sin by remembering the work of the triune God. The passage surrounding today's verse tells us that we are chosen by the Father, redeemed by the blood of the Son, and sanctified by the Spirit (see 1 Peter 1:1–5). Additionally, we are equipped to respond humbly to trials when we cherish the great inheritance reserved for us in heaven (see vv. 6–12). In verse 13, Peter begins to apply this doctrine to life. Godliness requires spiritual readiness, which means we need to be mentally prepared, alert, and hopeful for the return of Jesus Christ. Peter elaborates on three traits of readiness.

Spiritual alertness involves preparing our minds "for action." The word translated *preparing* means "gathering up"; some Bible translations use the word *girding*. In those days, people of the East wore long, loose robes that they gathered into their belts when preparing for physical activity. Peter is focused on the battlefield of our minds—he wants us to be ready. The apostle Paul shares the same concern. Near the end of his description of the armor of God, which we are to take up in our spiritual war, he exhorts us this way: "Stand therefore, having girded your waist with truth" (Eph. 6:14 NKJV). To win the war, your thinking must be fortified by the truth.

Spiritual alertness includes being "sober-minded." When people turn away from habitual overconsumption of alcohol, we describe them as becoming "sober" because their minds are no longer controlled by liquor. Instead, they are calm, collected, and in control. Peter calls you to practice spiritual sobriety as you resist Satan: "Be sober-minded; be watchful. Your adversary the devil prowls around like a roaring lion, seeking someone to devour" (1 Peter 5:8). A mind that is constantly renewed by the Word of truth will be sober and watchful—a strong defense against Satan's deception.

Spiritual alertness includes fixing our "hope fully on the grace" *of Jesus.* His grace, which is being brought to us now through the riches of redemption, will be revealed in its fullness at his coming. Unbelievers are not interested in looking for Jesus's return, but, by transforming grace, we "are not of the night or of the darkness. So then let us not sleep, as others do, but let us keep awake and be sober" (1 Thess. 5:5–6). We don't want Jesus to return to find us drunk with the wine of worldly thinking!

Our hearts are "deceitful above all things" (Jer. 17:9). Therefore, Scripture must be the final, trustworthy, objective test of the acceptability of our thoughts (Ps. 19:14). We need to stay awake.

TALK TO YOURSELF. Read James 3:13–18. In your journal, make a chart comparing human wisdom to God's wisdom. Take notice of the role of the devil in the arena of human wisdom.

TALK TO GOD. Pray through Psalm 19:14. Consider memorizing this verse so that it may become one of your regular prayers to grow in truth-saturated thinking.

TALK TO OTHERS. Ask a pastor, a mentor, or a mature believer to share with you some ways their thinking has changed because of spending regular time in the Word.

53. A Trinity of Grace

*For the grace of God has appeared, bringing salvation
for all people, training us to renounce ungodliness and
worldly passions, and to live self-controlled, upright, and
godly lives in the present age, waiting for our blessed hope,
the appearing of the glory of our great God and Savior
Jesus Christ. (Titus 2:11–13)*

The first stanza of one of the best-known Christian hymns is rightly cherished. "Amazing grace, how sweet the sound that saved a wretch like me. I once was lost but now am found, was blind but now I see." Equally important, but not as well known, is the second stanza: "'Twas grace that taught my heart to fear, and grace my fears relieved. How precious did that grace appear the hour I first believed."[3] Grace, the active love of God that led him to rescue us from everlasting condemnation, also teaches us to fear the Lord—that is, to realign our hearts with the precepts of his Word.

---

3. John Newton, "Amazing Grace," 1772.

As followers of Jesus, we readily admit that we're saved from our wretched, lost, and blind condition by God's grace alone. Yet too often we fail to understand, acknowledge, or fully appreciate how the grace that came to us "the hour [we] first believed" continues to carry us through the Christian life—from conversion all the way to glorification. Perhaps when John Newton penned his timeless hymn, he was thinking about the divine provision that today's verses reveal.

Titus 2:11–12 presents grace as our personal trainer that helps us to grow in our exercise of godliness. Negatively, grace trains us to "renounce ungodliness and worldly passions." Positively, grace trains us to "live self-controlled, upright, and godly lives." God saves us by his grace, but by that same grace he also disciplines us to become holy as our Savior is holy. Take a moment to think about the past, present, and future grace that is yours in Christ.

In Christ, you have already experienced the *past grace* of God, which "has appeared, bringing salvation for all [kinds of] people." Paul is not teaching universalism, that all people will eventually be saved. Instead, he focuses on how the Son of God came to save all kinds of sinners, who are trapped in all kinds of sins, and who come from all kinds of backgrounds and ethnicities. One day all those whom Jesus ransomed by his blood, "from every tribe and language and people and nation," will sing a new salvation song (Rev. 5:9).

In Christ, you experience the ongoing "training" of *present grace*. Well-meaning critics may say that thinking too much about grace will cause Christians to sin more, but biblical grace doesn't lead to licentiousness (see Rom. 6:1–2). The problem stems not from thinking *too much* about grace but from thinking *wrongly* about it. God's grace holds your hand while guiding you away from sinful longings and toward godly living "in the present age." Godliness is a foretaste of the future consummation of your redemption.

In Christ, you possess *future grace*, which will be fully realized when the Lord Jesus returns. In the meantime, the Spirit will not stop instructing you while you are "waiting for [your] blessed hope." This hope is the confident expectation that God will keep every promise made to you in Christ and by his grace bring you to the finale at "the appearing of the glory" of Christ. Keeping your eyes fixed on Jesus's return will benefit your sanctification, as John writes: "Everyone who thus hopes in him purifies himself as he is pure" (1 John 3:3).

As followers of Christ who are pursuing holiness, we may be confident that our sanctification will one day be complete. We will stand face to face with Jesus. We "know that when he appears we shall be like him, because we shall see him as he is" (1 John 3:2).

TALK TO YOURSELF. Say to yourself, "I am saved from sin and condemnation solely by the grace of God. But, even now, by the power of the Spirit within me, this same grace is training me to grow in holiness as I discipline myself and wait with expectancy for Jesus to return."

TALK TO GOD: Pray something like this: "Lord, thank you for saving my soul and forgiving my sin. But also thank you for not leaving me to fend for myself in the war against indwelling sin. Help me to humbly work in cooperation with the sanctifying grace of your Spirit."

TALK TO OTHERS: Is there another believer who may profit from what you've learned today about the "trinity of grace"? Perhaps call them or text Titus 2:11–13 to them along with a brief testimony of how this truth strengthens you in the fight.

54. Wash Away Your Old Ways of Thinking

*I appeal to you therefore, brothers and sisters, by the mercies
of God, to present your bodies as a living sacrifice, holy
and acceptable to God, which is your spiritual worship. Do
not be conformed to this world, but be transformed by the
renewal of your mind, that by testing you may discern what
is the will of God, what is good and acceptable and perfect.
(Rom. 12:1–2)*

What comes to mind when you hear the word *worldliness*? Is it a
certain behavior, a form of media or entertainment, or perhaps
the personal practice of another Christian that differs from your
own conviction? Rightly understood, worldliness is a misuse of
the Christian mind. The antidote is to renew your mind with
God's truth.

Instead of slothfully conforming our minds to think like the
rest of the world, we must discipline ourselves to think God's
thoughts according to his Word. The Scripture above begins with
an urgent request. That is, considering "the mercies of God" that
bring redemption to sinners (explained in Romans 1–11), Paul
urges us to present our bodies "as a living sacrifice." This is a passion-
ate plea for us to offer ourselves to God as we take up the vocation
of holiness. This appeal is logical: since God saved us, he owns
us, and his Spirit indwells us (see 1 Cor. 6:19–20). Our bodily
sacrifice is living, unlike the offerings of the Old Testament, all of
which were killed. However, for our "spiritual worship" to glorify
God, it must meet his holy standard, which has both negative and
positive aspects.

153

It is negative. "Do not be conformed to this world," the apostle urges. The word *conform* means to mold after something else. You should view this not merely as a warning to beware the world's attempt to shape you into its mold but as an admonition to avoid the temptation to pattern yourself after the world by adopting its values, priorities, and attitudes—its manner of thinking. Jesus died to deliver you from "the present evil age" (Gal. 1:4). To adopt its mindset is not an appropriate response to God's grace.

It is positive. God wants disciples of Jesus to "be transformed." *Transformed* comes from the same word from which we get *metamorphosis.* This transformation is a fundamental change of character and conduct away from the standards of the world and toward Christlikeness. You are set apart. You will not be transformed into the image of Christ without "the renewal of your mind."

Renewing our minds means washing out the worldly ways of thinking by filling ourselves with God's way of thinking. Picture a glass of dirty water. As we pour purified water into the glass, the dirty water is forced out. In a similar way, as we meditate on the Word of God, we are sanctified "by the washing of water with the word" (Eph. 5:26).

TALK TO YOURSELF. Employing another water illustration, Lydia Brownback writes, "The more we soak ourselves in God's Word, the more we will be able to readily lay hold of the wisdom we need for particular circumstances."[4] This reinforces our need to get into a consistent habit of Bible reading and meditation. What changes does the Spirit want you to make to renew your mind more consistently?

---

4. Lydia Brownback, *A Woman's Wisdom: How the Book of Proverbs Speaks to Everything* (Wheaton, IL: Crossway, 2012), 25.

TALK TO GOD. Journal a prayer that expresses the following: a desire to be conformed to Christ rather than the world, a resolve to spend more time in God's Word, and a willingness to do God's will.

TALK TO OTHERS. If you feel defeated over not developing consistent Bible reading habits, ask a mature Christian for help and accountability.

55. Meditate on the Word

This Book of the Law shall not depart from your mouth, but you shall meditate on it day and night, so that you may be careful to do according to all that is written in it. For then you will make your way prosperous, and then you will have good success. (Josh. 1:8)

Blessed is the man who walks not in the counsel of the wicked, nor stands in the way of sinners, nor sits in the seat of scoffers; but his delight is in the law of the LORD, and on his law he meditates day and night. (Ps. 1:1–2)

Our minds are prone to wander, and we are easily distracted. Therefore, if we are going to renew our minds with God's wisdom, we must learn to practice biblical meditation. But what does it mean to meditate? Meditation is a religious practice in many cultures and is even widely adopted by the secular world. Unfortunately, it is often thought of as *emptying* our minds. But, biblically speaking, nothing could be further from the truth. Meditation involves *filling* our minds with God's thoughts.

The Hebrew word used in both Joshua 1:8 and Psalm 1:2 carries the idea of *speaking to oneself*. To meditate, then, means to ponder something—to think deeply about a particular truth until it becomes internalized. Joshua and the author of Psalm 1 agree: meditating on the law of the Lord is a trademark of the "blessed" person who experiences "good success" in the eyes of the Lord.

Biblical meditation is the practice of mulling God's truth over and over in our minds "day and night" until it grips our hearts. The Puritan Thomas Watson explained it this way: "Without meditation the truth of God will not stay with us; the heart is hard, and the memory slippery, and without meditation all is lost; meditation imprints and fastens a truth in the mind. . . . As a hammer drives a nail to the head, so meditation drives a truth to the heart."[5] Through biblical meditation the Spirit grips our hearts and transforms our lives from the inside out.

Psalm 1 highlights this transformation by explaining the essential difference between the godly and the wicked: their hearts' affection. In other words, experiencing a blessed life is directly connected to having a right attitude toward the Scriptures, which in turn leads you to obey God in faith. This involves two ongoing disciplines of the mind.

Stay away from ungodly counsel. The wisdom of the world leads down the predictable path of moral compromise (walking leads to standing, which results in sitting down). These downward steps are illustrated in the choices of Abraham's nephew. It began when Lot lifted his eyes toward the fertile valley where the city of Sodom was located (see Gen. 13:10). Next, he moved into the valley and pitched his tent toward Sodom (see v. 12). Finally, he settled in Sodom itself (see Gen. 14:12). In the language of the psalmist, he

---

5. Quoted in David W. Saxton, *God's Battle Plan for the Mind: The Puritan Practice of Biblical Meditation* (Grand Rapids: Reformation Heritage Books, 2015), 6.

started *walking* "in the counsel of the wicked." Then he *stood* "in the way of sinners," and finally he *sat* among the "scoffers." If you don't consciously avoid the devil's lies, which are often concealed within unbiblical counsel, you may find yourself in a similar place.

Savor God's Word. Godliness consists of more than what you stay away from; it's about what you treasure. When your "delight is in the law of the Lord," you will desire to meditate on its beautiful truth, and you will be fruitful and stable (see Ps. 1:3). You experience abundant fruitfulness and oak-like stability in the Christian life in direct proportion to the extent to which you meditate on God's Word.

TALK TO YOURSELF. Your heart follows your treasure (see Luke 12:34). The more you treasure God's precepts by delighting in them, the more your heart will, in time, align with the wisdom and will of God. What do you need to do to grow in the discipline of Bible meditation?

TALK TO GOD. Before you read your Bible, begin getting in the habit of praying something like this: "Lord, I want to delight in your Word so that the treasures of my heart begin to conform to your desires and ways."

TALK TO OTHERS. Ask a friend in Christ or your small group leader (if you have one) to memorize Psalm 1 alongside you. Then discuss the ways you see the Spirit changing you.

REDIRECTING THE WILL

56. Choose the Pathway of Humility

Do nothing from selfish ambition or conceit, but in humility count others more significant than yourselves. (Phil. 2:3)

God's economy of glory is the opposite of ours. For example, if we want to rise to a higher rung on the corporate ladder, we climb—and may keep climbing even if we must step on others to get there. But Jesus says, "Whoever exalts himself will be humbled, and whoever humbles himself will be exalted" (Matt. 23:12). Or, if we want to sit in the most important chair at the banquet, our self-centered nature impels us toward the head of the table. But in God's system, the way up is not up. It's down. The person who sits in the most obscure chair gets seated in the chief place (see Luke 14:7–10). The one who becomes "the servant of all" will one day be the most important in the kingdom of God (see Mark 10:43–44).

This up-is-down principle is most visible in the Lord Jesus's attitudes and actions, and, as we are being remade in his likeness, our hearts must embrace this fundamental posture. However, humility doesn't come easily. Our pride works against the Spirit's cultivation of Christlike humility in us.

Pride is self-focused and self-serving; it's always jockeying itself into the best position to receive the most glory. We must resist pride by dying to ourselves: death is the pathway to humility, and humility is the pathway to Christlikeness.

That is the crux of the apostle's charge to us in today's Scripture reading. In the context of this verse, Paul roots Christian humility in the self-humiliation of Christ. We make humility our new disposition not by looking inward at our faults and failures but by looking to Jesus.

Humility begins in your mind but is activated by your will. Paul sandwiches his call to humility between two exhortations: to be of "the same mind, maintaining the same love" toward one another, and to have the "attitude" of Christ (Phil. 2:2, 5 NASB).

What was that attitude? Before the eternal Son of God humbled himself to be conceived by the Holy Spirit in the virgin's womb and born into our broken world, he considered our need of salvation to be greater than his right to always display his glory and, therefore, clothed himself in "the form of a bond-servant" (Phil. 2:7 NASB). Jesus resisted any path that moved him even one baby step toward self-glory. For you, then, being remade in Christ entails putting on the same mind by considering others "as more important" than yourself and looking out for "the interests of others" (v. 4 –5 NASB).

Humility will lead you to lower yourself while entrusting your future exaltation to God. Humble people are content with the absence of earthly recognition because they consider their heavenly glory to be infinitely superior. Jesus refused to consider his personal glory "a thing to be grasped" (Phil. 2:6). The word *grasp* means to hold to something so tightly that you could never let it go. He "emptied himself" (v. 7) by *taking on* something foreign to his divine nature—the weakness of human flesh. He subjected himself to the humiliation of public torture by "becoming obedient to the point of death, even death on a cross" (v. 8). Humility delayed his future glory, but it will be recognized one day, when "every knee [shall] bow, in heaven and on earth and under the earth, and every tongue confess that Jesus Christ is Lord, to the glory of God the Father" (vv. 10–11).

TALK TO YOURSELF. Andrew Murray writes, "Humility is the only soil in which the graces root; the lack of humility is the sufficient explanation of every defect and failure. Humility is not so much a grace or virtue along with others; it is the root of all."[1] Do you see this connection in your life? Do you see how humility aids growth in Christlikeness? Are there any ways you see pride hindering your growth?

TALK TO GOD. Proverbs 8:13 says, "The fear of the LORD is hatred of evil. Pride and arrogance and the way of evil and perverted speech I hate." Confess to God the ways you see pride evident in your life and ask him to help you to fear him above all.

TALK TO OTHERS. Ask a mature Christian who knows you well to point out evidence of humility in your life as well as areas where you may be blinded to your own pride.

1. Andrew Murray, *Humility* (1884; repr., Springdale, PA: Whitaker House, 1982), 12.

57. Don't Forget to Put on a Belt

And above all these put on love, which binds everything together in perfect harmony. (Col. 3:14)

My parents were attentive to how their six children dressed when we went out in public. They were not excessively picky or smothering, but they wanted us to appear shipshape. For example, when we were getting ready for school or church, Mom or Dad would typically say, "Don't forget to put on a belt." Why did they do this? A belt finished off the outfit. It tidied up our appearance and held everything together.

The same is true of Christlike love. Love is the belt that ties all the Christian virtues together. That's the apostle's point in today's verse. The command to "put on love" is located near the end of a running list of exhortations to "God's chosen ones, holy and beloved" (Col. 3:12) to "put on the new self" (v. 10).

To help us get practical, consider that *put on* may also be translated "clothe." This change in our wardrobe, however, isn't about improving our outward appearance. It involves throwing away the clothing of the old man: the sins of the flesh, such as "anger, wrath, malice, slander, and obscene talk" as well as lies (Col. 3:8–9). In place of our old attire, we must put on the new wardrobe of Christlikeness, which includes "compassionate hearts, kindness, humility, meekness, and patience" as well as forbearance and forgiveness (v. 12; see also v. 13). Through the heart-transforming power of the gospel, the Holy Spirit aims to give us an extreme makeover—to empty the closet of our old ways and give us a new wardrobe. And the belt that "binds everything together in perfect harmony" is love.

Love is all-encompassing. "Owe no one anything, except to love each other," Paul writes to the church at Rome (Rom. 13:8). Here, Paul draws attention to the superiority and permanent impact of love, "for the one who loves another has fulfilled the law" (v. 8). In other words, the one debt we will never be free from is the debt of love.

This agrees with Jesus's teaching concerning the two supreme commandments: to love God and others ties together all the rest of God's commandments (see Matt. 22: 37–40). If we *always* love God with all our hearts, souls, and minds, and if we *always* love our neighbors as ourselves, we will never sin. "Love does no wrong to a neighbor; therefore love is the fulfilling of the law" (Rom 13:10).

The belt of love is woven together with cords of humility. To love biblically is to consider others to be more important than yourself. Love is the culmination of all other virtues because its selflessness brings glory to our humble Savior. When we tie our new wardrobe together with demonstrations of Christ's love, we will find ourselves becoming more like our Savior.

TALK TO YOURSELF. "Let all that you do be done in love" (1 Cor. 16:14). How does this verse speak to your current relationships? Consider memorizing it so that the Spirit may more easily bring it to mind when a "love choice" needs to be made.

TALK TO GOD. To the believers in Thessalonica, the apostle wrote, "Now concerning brotherly love you have no need for anyone to write to you, for you yourselves have been taught by God to love one another" (1 Thess. 4:9). In what ways do your attitudes and actions toward others lack Christlike love? Ask the Lord to forgive you for these sins of omission and to teach you to grow in love.

TALK TO OTHERS. How can you practically express selfless love to someone this week?

58. Run Together

*Therefore, since we are surrounded by so great a cloud of
witnesses, let us also lay aside every weight, and sin which
clings so closely, and let us run with endurance the race that
is set before us, looking to Jesus, the founder and perfecter of
our faith, who for the joy that was set before him endured
the cross, despising the shame, and is seated at the right
hand of the throne of God. (Heb. 12:1–2)*

At the 2020 Olympic Games in Tokyo, Ethiopian-born Sifan
Hassan made history. Running for the Netherlands, the twenty-
eight-year-old overcame every obstacle to become the first woman
to win three distance medals at an Olympic game. Famous for her
speed, Sifan is also known for preferring to hang back and then
burst ahead in the final lap. One of the most amazing moments
in the games was when she tripped over another runner who had
fallen. Sifan got back up and blasted past eleven runners to take
the gold medal.

One word describes this world-renowned athlete: *endurance*.
Yet it's important to note that the endurance she displayed came
from being part of a team. Sifan was part of Team Netherlands.
She ran *for* them and *with* them; she did not run alone. We too
need to run alongside others if we are going to finish the Christian race well.

The author of the book of Hebrews writes to Christians as a
team, not as individuals. In fact, in today's verses alone, he uses
plural pronouns five times. Read the verses again and notice the
use of *we, us,* and *our.* Endurance requires team effort. Every one

of us must stay in the race. None of us has the privilege of sitting on the bleachers while our teammates run for Christ. But how will we endure? We have three ongoing disciplines to practice.

Fellowship with faithful believers both past and present. Having described many faithful men and women in Hebrews 11, the hall of faith, the writer to the Hebrews now informs us that we are "surrounded by so great a cloud of witnesses." These believers who have gone on to glory testify of God's faithfulness and are examples of endurance. We fellowship with believers who lived in the recent past by reading Christian biographies, and in biblical history by reading Scripture, which was written "for our instruction, that through endurance and through the encouragement of the Scriptures we might have hope" (Rom. 15:4). We also grow in endurance by running with other believers in the present, as we practice the regular rhythm of worship and service in our local church family (see Heb. 10:24–25).

Fight for godliness while tackling our sins and growing in endurance. Remember, godliness is always a both/and endeavor. We must "lay aside every weight," which includes what may be harmless or otherwise useful but still drags us down. And we need to put off the "sin which clings so closely." Again, we are most effective at fleeing sin and pursuing righteousness "along with those who call on the Lord from a pure heart" (2 Tim. 2:22). We will never win alone.

Focus on Jesus and his priestly work, both past and present. The word *looking* may be translated "fixing," which means to look away from one thing so that we can look intently at something else. We must habitually look away from sin toward Christ. He is "the founder and perfecter of our faith," and we must focus our attention on his sacrificial work in the past, when he "endured the cross" while "despising the shame." Jesus endured by fixing his attention on "the joy that was set before him," the joy of one day sharing his glory with those whom he came to redeem. But we also focus on his present work at the right hand of God, where he is currently interceding for us (see Rom. 8:34).

God placed every follower of Jesus in the race; sitting out is not an option. Be encouraged! You are not running alone.

TALK TO YOURSELF. Read Colossians 3:8–14. What sins or weights do you need to lay aside?

TALK TO GOD. Confess your weights and besetting sins to God. Ask the Spirit to grow your endurance.

TALK TO OTHERS. You are not running the Christian race alone. Therefore, who can you reach out to for help this week? Who is discouraged and needs your help? Reach out to them.

59. Bear One Another's Sin Burdens

Brothers and sisters, if anyone is caught in any transgression,
you who are spiritual should restore him in a spirit of
gentleness. Keep watch on yourself, lest you too be tempted.
Bear one another's burdens, and so fulfill the law of Christ.
(Gal. 6:1–2)

As we learned in the last reading, God never intended for any of us to run the Christian race alone. Today, we need to consider how Christian love works when a fellow runner falls and cannot get back up. Thankfully, God intends for the church to look more like a hospital for failing sinners than a country club for flawless saints. In Christ, we are saints, yes, but until our spirits leave our fallen bodies, we will battle the world, the flesh, and the devil.

As we wait for the day when we will see our glorified Savior, we have a responsibility to help those who are losing the battle against besetting sin. Paul describes this one-another ministry in Galatians 6:1–5 and includes support and accountability for fellow believers who find themselves "caught in any transgression." Our duty is clear: "Bear one another's burdens, and so fulfill the law of Christ." A *burden* in this context is the weight of sin or the burden of temptation that has trapped a brother or sister in the Lord. To bear their burden is to help them to overcome their sin.

Nevertheless, though you who are "spiritual" are responsible for carrying the burden *with* those who are trapped, you do not carry it *for* them: "Each will have to bear his own load" (Gal. 6:5). The help you give to a defeated brother or sister does not remove an ounce of their personal responsibility. They are still, first and foremost, morally accountable to God as creatures made in his image and children redeemed by the Son.

We are to lovingly confront our spiritual siblings while keeping the goal of restoration in view. We remind the one who is caught in sin that "the law of the Spirit of life has set you free in Christ Jesus from the law of sin and death" (Rom. 8:2). By ministering in this way, we "fulfill the law of Christ," who came not to be served but to serve (see Mark 10:45).

We are called to "walk in love" (Eph. 5:2) as we look to the long-term good of our brothers and sisters. We must love one another enough to humbly confront those who are trapped by sin and gently lead them onto the path of righteousness. Our ministry to restore the fallen within the church should be marked by grace, compassion, and truth.

Love grows from the root of humility: we must remember that we ourselves are vulnerable. And, at the same time, as believers committed to one another's spiritual well-being, we recognize that we are not the only ones fighting the daily battle against sin. Our brothers and sisters are too. Some may be losing the war and need extra help to gain victory.

TALK TO YOURSELF. When God asked Cain where Abel was, he replied, "Am I my brother's keeper?" (Gen. 4:9). When you see a brother or sister entrapped in sin, are you tempted to respond in a similar way? Do you think, "That's none of my business," or "It's their life, not mine"?

TALK TO GOD. Journal a list of the ways other believers have come alongside to exhort, encourage, and help you in times of struggle. Thank God for their courage and selfless love for you.

TALK TO OTHERS. How could a better understanding of Galatians 6:1–2 shape your actions today? How might God want you to carry out this one-another responsibility out of love for a brother or sister caught in sin?

60. Stay Out of the Ditches

Therefore, my beloved, as you have always obeyed, so now,
not only as in my presence but much more in my absence,
work out your own salvation with fear and trembling, for
it is God who works in you, both to will and to work for his
good pleasure. (Phil. 2:12–13)

While a sophomore in high school, I learned to drive my dad's
1973 Pontiac Catalina. I confess, its 400-cubic-inch, eight-cylinder
engine was more than a little fun at times, although driving on
winter roads in Wisconsin was challenging. As I would leave for
work, it wasn't uncommon for Mom or Dad to say, "Stay out of the
ditches." As Christ followers, we also need to stay out of ditches.
We need to watch out for theological extremes that hinder our
progress on Sanctification Road.

As we come to the end of part 2, it's imperative for you to
wholeheartedly embrace cooperative sanctification—that is, to
take hold of your duty to discipline yourself for godliness *while*
at the same time relying on the power of the Holy Spirit to work
in you. Without this biblical balance, you will drift toward one of
two extremes and may end up in a ditch.

The first extreme is quietism. Quietists believe the will of the
Christian is quiet, or passive, in sanctification. But this is incorrect:
the Spirit doesn't transform you while you simply "let go and let
God." The second extreme is pietism. Pietists believe their spiritual
growth rests entirely on their own shoulders. This often results in
a legalistic reliance on keeping the law. Today's Scripture helps
you to guard against these errors by balancing two essential truths.

You are responsible for your spiritual growth. Philippians 2:12
begins with the word *therefore,* which links back to a prior empha-
sis on the lordship of Christ (see vv. 9–11). Paul commends his
readers for having "always obeyed" not only in his "presence but

much more in [his] absence." Then he gives them (and us) this admonition: "Work out your own salvation." The apostle is not urging believers to work *for* salvation, since salvation is by grace alone, but to work *out* (or outwardly) the inner change of heart that the Spirit has accomplished through the gospel. In other words, you need to make every effort to complete your faith "with fear and trembling." You need a healthy concern for your growth in Christ. However, yet another truth balances out our response to this command.

You are dependent on God for your spiritual growth. Though you're responsible to discipline yourself for godliness, it's also true that you are powerless to make any lasting change on your own. The good news is that God "works in you, both to will and to work for his good pleasure." As the Spirit sanctifies you by means of his Word and his people, he reorients your will to the will of God as he creates new desires in you—all for God's "good pleasure." The empowering presence of the Spirit will bring to completion the good work that God began in you (see Phil. 1:6).

We all tend to veer toward spiritual extremes and, therefore, need to keep these balancing truths in mind. Let's not be spiritual sluggards who put forth little effort to become godly. But let's also not assume that our progress is completely dependent on our own efforts. Ultimately, the Spirit of God bears fruit in us for God's glory. We need to rest in his strength, and we also need to ask for help from others when we need it as well as to come alongside others in turn.

TALK TO YOURSELF. Which ditch are you most likely to fall into? Are you more prone to spiritual apathy or to self-confidence in your ability to fight sin?

TALK TO GOD. In your own words, journal today's verses in the form of a prayer of thanksgiving. Request God's help as you walk along Sanctification Road.

TALK TO OTHERS. Seek out another believer in your church and discuss how you can help each other to balance these two essential truths.

SUFFERER

SUBMITTING TO YOUR PURIFICATION IN CHRIST

The purpose of part 3 is to help you to learn not only to accept suffering but to embrace it as one of the primary tools that God uses to work out your sanctification in Christ and to appreciate God's loving presence and care throughout your life.

DON'T BE SURPRISED
BY SUFFERING

61. You Are Called to Suffer with Christ

For to this you have been called, because Christ also suffered
for you, leaving you an example, so that you might follow in
his steps. (1 Peter 2:21)

Several years ago, one of our daughters asked why our family seems
to suffer more than other people she knows who do not follow
the Lord. "Sometimes," she said, "it seems life would be easier if
we weren't Christians." It can feel like that sometimes, can't it?
Jesus predicted that all who follow him will suffer: "In the world
you will have tribulation" (John 16:33). Yet he urges us to "take
heart" since he has already "overcome the world" (v. 33). Today's
Scripture reading clarifies that suffering is part of our calling as
Christ-followers. The context of this admonition is suffering for
righteousness' sake—that is, persecution for doing right. However,
the same truth serves as an umbrella principle over all forms of
suffering we endure. Simply put, we are *sufferers*.

Our new identity in Christ is first and foremost that of saints. As saints, we still wrestle indwelling sin, as we saw in part 2. As saints, we also endure a lot of suffering in this world. This is the final lens we will look through to get a wide-angle view of God's sanctifying work in us.

We were born into a world that God cursed when humanity first sinned against him in the garden of Eden (Gen. 3:17). As a result, we groan. We groan because life hurts badly—sometimes with unspeakable sorrows. But, unlike those who do not know Jesus, we groan with hope. We groan *while* we wait for the ultimate day of redemption when "the creation itself will be set free from its bondage to corruption" (Rom. 8:21). We groan as our hearts ache for the day when Jesus will make "all things new" (Rev. 21:5). Until then, suffering is guaranteed.

Don't misunderstand me, and do not forget. Your primary Christian identity is exalted and victorious. You are united with Christ. You have received his righteousness in exchange for your sin. God sees you as though you *already* are seated in the heavens and possess every spiritual blessing (see Eph. 1:3). Make no mistake: your eternal inheritance is more glorious than you can imagine. Still, you live in a world of pain, anguish, and loss.

Suffering is both common to all human beings and more severe for Christians due to our union with the suffering Savior. Yet the suffering we experience is unlike Jesus's in one very significant way: his suffering atoned for sin; ours never could. Jesus alone is the Lamb of God who takes away the sins of the world (see John 1:29). Jesus—and only Jesus—could be the "once for all" sacrifice foreshadowed by the Old Testament (Heb. 7:27; 9:12; see also 1 Peter 3:18). He is the "one mediator between God and men" (1 Tim. 2:5). He alone is Savior (see Acts 4:12).

Your suffering could never atone for your sin and, therefore, can never save you. But that is good news, since that is not its purpose! Jesus "suffered for you." You don't have to pay for your sin because Jesus already did. Instead, your suffering has a sanctifying purpose: to make you holy and deepen your relationship with Jesus (see Phil. 3:10).

Jesus will teach you how to endure suffering with joy since he left you "an example," so that you might "follow in his steps." As you follow him and rely on his strengthening grace, your suffering bonds you to him and conforms you to his image.

TALK TO YOURSELF. Prior to reading today's meditation, how did you think about your suffering as a Christian? David Powlison explains the connection between your sainthood and your suffering this way: "God calls you a saint to point out who owns you, not to honor you for going above and beyond the call of duty. It's not the Medal of Honor. It's your enlistment papers and dog tag. When God has written his name on you, suffering qualitatively changes."[1] Consider this explanation and how it might be a comfort to you.

TALK TO GOD. Pray through 1 Peter 2:18–25, asking God to strengthen you to follow the example of Christ, who suffered unjustly yet "continued entrusting himself to him who judges justly" (v. 23).

TALK TO OTHERS. Reach out to a member of your church whom you have watched endure an extended time of suffering. Let them know some ways their Christlike example has encouraged your spiritual growth.

---

1. David Powlison, *God's Grace in Your Suffering* (Wheaton, IL: Crossway, 2018), 35.

62. Proven Faith Is More Precious than Gold

In this you rejoice, though now for a little while, if necessary,
you have been grieved by various trials, so that the tested
genuineness of your faith—more precious than gold that
perishes though it is tested by fire—may be found to result in
praise and glory and honor at the revelation of Jesus Christ.
(1 Peter 1:6–7)

The simple gold ring on my left hand is priceless to me. It is my most valuable piece of jewelry because it symbolizes God's gracious gift of a faithful wife. Originally, it belonged to another man, my wife's great-grandfather, but was given to my wife by her grandmother when we got engaged. Karen took it to a local jeweler to get it resized so she could place it on my finger on our wedding day. Yet, as valuable as the gold used to make this ring may be, there is something else that is more precious and valued: faith that is tested by fire and proven to be genuine.

Commentator Kenneth Wuest explains the apostle's illustration of an ancient goldsmith, who

> refines the crude gold ore in his crucible. The pure metal is mixed with much foreign material from which it must be separated. The only way to bring about this separation is to reduce the ore to liquid form. The impurities rise to the surface and are then skimmed off. But intense heat is needed to liquefy this ore. So the goldsmith puts his crucible in the fire, reduces the ore to a liquid state and skims off the impurities. When he can see the reflection

of his face clearly mirrored in the surface of the liquid, he knows that the contents are pure gold. The smelting process has done its work.[2]

In the same way, the divine Goldsmith turns up the thermostat of our lives to sanctify us. He heats up the smelting furnace of affliction to reveal imperfections in our hearts so they can be skimmed off by our confession and repentance. Today's Scripture reading makes it clear that God does this not to defeat us but to prove the "genuineness" of our faith.

This was the case with Job, an Old Testament hero of the faith. God brought Job to the devil's attention: "Have you considered my servant Job, that there is none like him on the earth, a blameless and upright man, who fears God and turns away from evil?" (Job 1:8). Satan is not coequal with God. He is a finite creature who is accountable to the Creator. Even though the devil meant his attacks for evil, God meant them for good.

Job understood the process Peter describes. The furnace was turned up to very hot when God permitted Satan to attack Job's family, health, financial security, and reputation. When Satan's tsunami came ashore, Job fell in broken, submissive worship (1:20). When blistering heat revealed Job's pride, Job confessed and repented (see Job 38–39). On the other side of his tragedy and trauma, Job spoke well of God: "When he has tried me, I shall come out [of the smelting pot] as gold" (23:10). Through it all, Job's faith was tested and proven genuine; his suffering accomplished its intended purposes.

Be encouraged! God is up to something good amid your pain. As the refiner's fire removes impurities to bring out the beauty of gold, so God uses trials to refine and bring out the beauty of your

2. Kenneth S. Wuest, *Bypaths*, in *Wuest's Word Studies from the Greek New Testament for the English Reader* (Grand Rapids: Wm. B. Eerdmans, 1973), 3:73.

faith. The Father looks to the heart that clings to him *while* faith is being refined and sees the image of his Son being revealed. In this, he is pleased and glorified.

TALK TO YOURSELF. How have you viewed trials in the past? Has today's meditation caused you to see them in a new light? How?

TALK TO GOD. Read Job 42:5. By the time his season of suffering ended, Job had gained a renewed awareness and deeper knowledge of God. Put this verse into your own words in the form of a prayer. Ask the Spirit to sanctify you through your suffering.

TALK TO OTHERS. The Puritan Samuel Rutherford wrote, "Grace withers without adversity. The devil is but God's master fencer to teach us to handle our weapons."[3] The devil is God's servant—have you ever considered what that means? God is never the source of evil, but he uses what the Evil One does against us to increase our spiritual fortitude in battle. Talk with another follower of Jesus about this mystery of God's providence. Together, thank the Lord for the increase of grace he gives to us in adversity.

3. *Letters of Samuel Rutherford: A Selection* (Edinburgh: Banner of Truth, 2015), 69, quoted in Dale W. Smith, ed., *Ore from the Puritans' Mine* (Grand Rapids: Reformation Heritage Books, 2020), 566.

63. The Whole Creation Suffers the Pain of Childbirth

For we know that the whole creation has been groaning together in the pains of childbirth until now. (Rom. 8:22)

On December 14, 2019, our sixth grandchild was born. The thirty-one weeks of life she enjoyed in the safety of her mother's womb continued for about forty-five minutes after birth. Then she was escorted into the arms of her Creator and Savior.

At eleven weeks' gestation, our daughter and son-in-law had learned of their firstborn's dire medical complications—complications that would make it impossible for her to survive outside the womb. When the expectation of miscarriage passed, her first-time parents named her Isabelle. At that point, their prayer requests became very specific—namely, that Isabelle would survive birth so her mom and dad could meet her while she was still alive. God answered these prayers. For three-quarters of an hour they snuggled with their little one and then placed her into the arms of Jesus. Even though we knew what was going to happen, it did not make the grief of her loss any easier. The death of a loved one—even when it is expected—can feel like a knockout punch.

In this valley of sorrow, the Spirit reminded me of how the Scriptures employ the imagery of childbirth to depict suffering in our broken world. In fact, today's verse informs us that ever since sin entered the garden of Eden, "the whole creation has been groaning together in the pains of childbirth." What sustains a woman through pregnancy and the pain of delivery is the anticipation of holding her precious child. Like expectant parents, we get strength for today by anchoring ourselves to the future hope revealed in Scripture. Whatever your circumstances or experience with grief, may your heart be strengthened by the following truths.

God ordains the length of each person's life, even before each one of us is born. "In your book were written, every one of them, the days that were formed for me, when as yet there was none of them" (Ps. 139:16). Every human life is of immeasurable value regardless of a person's abilities or disabilities, or how long they live, because every person is created in the image of God and our definite purpose is ordained by God.

Death is a defeated enemy. "Death is swallowed up in victory" (1 Cor. 15:54). Death is one consequence of the original sin that was engineered by the Enemy of our souls. The devil is a destroyer, but neither he nor death will get the final word. The devil's doom and death's end have already been sealed by Jesus (see Rev. 20:10; 21:4).

Grief hurts, but God's comfort is real. "Blessed be the God and Father of our Lord Jesus Christ, the Father of mercies and God of all comfort" (2 Cor. 1:3). The loss of loved ones hurts deeply, regardless of how or when it occurs. During these times, he is our merciful comforter. Yet God is not our only source of comfort. Even with his help, we are not strong enough to carry the burden of grief without the aid of other people. "Shared sorrow is endurable sorrow. We were never meant to suffer alone; we are meant to comfort and encourage one another."[4]

None of us can escape the pain of suffering. How crucial it is then that we develop a God-centered perspective on suffering: it is short-term compared to our everlasting joy in the presence of the Savior.

---

4. Bob Kellemen, *Grief: Walking with Jesus* (Phillipsburg, NJ: P&R Publishing, 2018), 14.

TALK TO YOURSELF. The comfort we receive from God, and through others, equips us to become more compassionate comforters ourselves. When you experience loss, do you tend to isolate yourself from others? If so, why do you think that is the case? Have you considered how the Lord might use you to comfort others who are hurting?

TALK TO GOD. Read Revelation 21:1–6 and then spend time thanking the Lord for your future hope in Christ.

TALK TO OTHERS. Shared grief has a way of strengthening God's church as a loving family. Is someone in your church family walking through grief right now? Reach out to them this week.

64. The Muscle of Your Faith Needs Exercise

Count it all joy, my brothers and sisters, when you meet trials of various kinds, for you know that the testing of your faith produces steadfastness. And let steadfastness have its full effect, that you may be perfect and complete, lacking in nothing. (James 1:2–4)

In *Trusting God*, Jerry Bridges describes the physical exertion of the Cecropia moth as it exits its cocoon. He then tells the story of a sympathetic viewer who snipped the shell of a cocoon to free a struggling moth. What this person did not understand "was that the struggle to emerge from the cocoon was an essential part of developing the muscle system of the moth's body and pushing the body fluids out into the wings to expand them. By unwisely seeking to cut short the moth's struggle, the watcher had actually crippled the moth and doomed its existence."[5]

Such is the case with the muscle of our faith. If we habitually seek to escape from all painful trials rather than joyfully submitting to them as part of God's endurance-building program, we may forgo opportunities to have our faith muscles exercised and strengthened.

In today's Scripture reading, James teaches us that knowing the goal of suffering is an important part of being able to "count it all joy" when we encounter "trials of various kinds." God tests our faith to produce steadfastness, or endurance. The word *steadfastness* comes from a compound word meaning to "stay under," "abide," or "remain." It's the picture of someone who has been carrying a heavy load for a long time, remaining under its weight instead of seeking to cast it off. Similarly, endurance develops when we remain under a trial while resisting the temptation to run from it. As we stick out our trials, our faith is strengthened. As Kent Hughes says, "The more tests we pass, the tougher we become."[6]

God's good purpose will often be accomplished as we humbly submit to our trials. God may remove the trial when we have learned what it was sent to teach us. Or it may be his will for us to remain under it indefinitely.[7] As we mature in Christ, we learn to remain under our trials until God lifts them or accomplishes their character-building purpose.

When suffering comes your way, you have two basic choices: You can choose to persevere under trial and grow in endurance,

---

5. Jerry Bridges, *Trusting God* (Colorado Springs: NavPress, 1988), 173–74.

6. R. Kent Hughes, *James: Faith That Works* (Wheaton, IL: Crossway Books, 1991), 19.

7. In the course of applying biblical wisdom, we may discern that God is leading us in another direction. For example, Proverbs 22:3 teaches that "the prudent sees danger and hides himself, but the simple go on and suffer for it." Generally speaking, however, it is healthy for us to avoid falling into escapist patterns.

or you can run from pain and be robbed of growth. One way you gain; the other way you lose. If you decide you've had enough pressure and develop the habit of running from all trials, you will short-circuit the process of your own spiritual maturity.

Steadfastness, as virtuous as it is, is not God's final goal. God doesn't want you merely to endure but to endure with joy—knowing his goal is to make you "perfect and complete, lacking in nothing." God's goal is to bring you to the finish line, whole and mature.

Spiritual maturity is what God is after in our trials. And if you want to know what spiritual maturity looks like, look at Jesus. You can be joyful in the midst of suffering when you know and embrace God's good purpose to develop your faith muscles in such a way that you reflect Christ.

TALK TO YOURSELF. Remind yourself that God in his goodness sends just the right trials at just the right time for you and your loved ones.

TALK TO GOD. Write a prayer of thanksgiving for the purpose of suffering. Ask God to give you a heart of humility to submit to your current trial.

TALK TO OTHERS. Ask a trusted believer to pray that God will grant you wisdom and endurance under trial. If you are unsure whether it is wise to remain under your current suffering or are wondering if God may want to use your bad situation to move you in another direction, seek counsel from a pastor, elder, or trustworthy Christian friend.

65. The Gift of Pain

*Three times I pleaded with the Lord about this, that it should
leave me. But he said to me, "My grace is sufficient for you,
for my power is made perfect in weakness." (2 Cor. 12:8)*

Gifts come wrapped in all kinds of packaging. Some are decorated
ornately with foil paper, sparkly ribbons, and ornaments. Others
are covered in much simpler wrapping. My wife, for example, wraps
gifts beautifully—with bows and ribbons and all—whereas I'm
content to use plain brown paper labeled with a black marker. No
matter how they look, however, gifts express their givers' intent
to be a blessing. In a similar way, suffering comes in various kinds
of packaging. It may be complicated by several interconnected
factors, or its one looming cause may be plain to see.

Either way, it's essential to view suffering as a gift from the
ultimate Giver whose love for us is profound and whose intent
is to bless. This was the apostle Paul's conclusion after God told
him no when he asked God to remove his pain. Three times, Paul
begged the Lord to take away his affliction. But instead of removing the thorn, Jesus replied, "My grace is sufficient for you, for my
power is made perfect in weakness." In short, he said, "No, Paul,
I will not take it from you." Jesus knew the revelation that Paul
received would tempt him to exalt himself. So, Paul's loving Lord
wrapped an unidentified thorn in the flesh, labeled it with Paul's
name and address, and had it delivered by Satan. This is important
to understand: no suffering enters your life apart from God's plan.
From Paul's experience, we learn that the gift of pain comes with
at least two benefits.

Pain fights pride and fosters humility. Paul confesses, "So to keep me from becoming conceited because of the surpassing greatness of the revelations, a thorn was given me" (2 Cor. 12:7). The uniqueness of Paul's celestial experience was sure to produce arrogance, which would hinder his usefulness. Pay attention. Physical and mental suffering may bless you by forcing you to depend upon God, thus bringing him more glory.

Pain underscores the sufficiency of Jesus. The Lord gave Paul his trial to demonstrate the power of grace. He said to Paul, "My grace is sufficient for you" (2 Cor. 12:9). Earlier, Paul wrote of the same empowering grace: "But by the grace of God I am what I am, and his grace toward me was not in vain" (1 Cor. 15:10). But now Paul has a deeper appreciation for Christ's sustaining grace. He understands that God's grace not only saves his saints from sin but also empowers them for service.

"My power is made perfect in weakness" means the power of Christ is brought to its calculated end through our weakness, not our strength. God designed it this way. The contrast of our weakness with God's power brings God the glory he deserves. Without Paul's thorn in the flesh, the glory of Christ would have been minimized by Paul's strength and pride. The same is true for you and me.

TALK TO YOURSELF. "Our physical illness is never simply a matter of germs and genetics," writes Megan Hill, but Scripture shows us "that our suffering is the careful tool of a loving God, designed for our good."[8] Do you think of suffering as a good gift from God? Why or why not?

8. Megan Hill, *Contentment: Seeing God's Goodness* (Phillipsburg, NJ: P&R Publishing, 2018), 81.

TALK TO GOD. Take a moment to thank God for one specific trial in your life and the ways the Spirit is employing it to strengthen you.

TALK TO OTHERS. Do you know brothers or sisters in the Lord who are suffering right now? Pray for them and then let them know you brought them to the throne of grace.

TRUSTING GOD

66. God Hears Your Groaning

Their cry for rescue from slavery came up to God. And God
heard their groaning, and God remembered his covenant
with Abraham, with Isaac, and with Jacob. God saw the
people of Israel—and God knew. (Ex. 2:23–25)

We verbalize our pain when we realize we need help. Otherwise,
we keep silent. Out of the pride of self-reliance or the pain of
having been ignored by others, we may decide to grit our teeth
or keep a stiff upper lip to get through pain alone, but that's rarely
healthy. God designed us to need others—most of all to need him.
He delights in tilting his head toward the groaning of his beloved
children. Nestled in today's verses are four poignant phrases that
reveal the Lord's heart for us when we hurt: "God heard their
groaning . . . God remembered his covenant. . . . God saw the
people . . . and God knew."

The first two chapters of Exodus set the stage. Many years have
passed since the book of Genesis ended with Jacob and his twelve
sons relocating to the opulent land of Egypt. There's been a major
change in national leadership, resulting in "a new king . . . who did
not know Joseph" (Ex. 1:8). Joseph, once revered by all and second

in command under Pharaoh, is now dead and forgotten, but the seed of Abraham has grown into a mighty nation, two million strong. Threatened by their power and controlled by his fear, the new leader puts Israel under his thumb by placing "taskmasters over them to afflict them with heavy burdens" (v. 11).

The people of God "were oppressed" (Ex. 1:12). This is the same word used in Genesis 15:13 to predict their enslavement in "the iron furnace" (Deut. 4:20) from which God would deliver them. "But the more they were oppressed, the more they multiplied and the more they spread abroad" (Ex. 1:12). So the king doubled down by adding extermination to his strategy: he commanded the Hebrew midwives to carry out gender-specific infanticide.

But the evil king was in for a surprise. The women feared God more than they feared him. So did Moses's parents. As a result, God's chosen deliverer was preserved: "By faith Moses, when he was born, was hidden for three months by his parents, because they saw that the child was beautiful, and they were not afraid of the king's edict" (Heb. 11:23).

The midwives, along with Moses's parents, had a living trust—faith that emboldened them to entrust themselves and their families to God in the face of great fear. In the end, God used the satanic murder of Hebrew children to move baby Moses into Pharaoh's house, where he would be raised in their customs and receive the best education the Egyptians had to offer. Thus, the Lord not only watched over him but, through him, watched over all his people.

We too may entrust ourselves to God's care. God sent Moses to deliver his chosen people from Egyptian bondage, and God did something infinitely greater when he gave his only begotten Son to deliver us from our slavery to sin. Jesus is the Promised Seed of Abraham (see Matt. 1:1) who secured our freedom. Because of him, we also have the everyday assurance that when we hurt, God hears our groaning. Whatever trials you may endure, whatever pain you may feel right now, know this: He hears your groanings.

He sees your pain. And he knows all about your situation. You can trust him to carry you through.

TALK TO YOURSELF. Ponder this Christ-centered reality: "He who did not spare his own Son but gave him up for us all, how will he not also with him graciously give us all things?" (Rom. 8:32).

TALK TO GOD. Read Psalm 121 and then pray through it in your own words.

TALK TO OTHERS. Read Psalm 37 with a friend. Discuss the ways you are assured of the Lord's attentive care and safekeeping.

67. Chronic Illness, Death, and the Compassionate Savior

She had heard the reports about Jesus and came up behind him in the crowd and touched his garment. For she said, "If I touch even his garments, I will be made well."
(Mark 5:27–28)

Our world is filled with all kinds of trouble and suffering. Therefore, it is a great comfort to know that we have Jesus as our refuge and heaven as our eternal resting place. Moreover, our Savior assures us that we don't have to wait until heaven to experience his compassion. Our Shepherd walks through our valleys of sorrow with us, for his heart is filled with compassion toward us.

In Mark 5:21–43, we catch a glimpse of the Savior's tender heart as he graciously serves different but equally needy people: a religious ruler and his wife, their twelve-year-old daughter, and a woman with an incurable disease. In each interaction, Jesus moves toward the helpless who approach him in childlike faith.

Gentle Jesus moves toward two very different members of society: one, an elite religious leader; the second, a social outcast. First, a ruler of the synagogue falls at Jesus's feet as a desperate, heartbroken father who is helpless to save his dying daughter. "Come and lay your hands on her, so that she may be made well and live," Jairus humbly pleads (v. 23).

Second, an unnamed woman suffering from unrelenting bleeding finds a glimmer of hope when she hears reports of Jesus. She's spent every penny she had on doctors who were as unhelpful as she was helpless (see vv. 24–26). On top of that, she is ceremonially unclean, alone, and unable to go to the temple for public worship (see Lev. 15). Her twelve-year quarantine has left her lonely and desperate. Yet she slowly makes her way through the crowd in hopes that she might be able to simply touch Jesus's cloak as he walks by.

The back-to-back order of these encounters sends a strong message: God is no respecter of persons. Anyone suffering from fear of death, chronic pain, or illness may come to him.

The faith of the bleeding woman is not sophisticated; it is simple. And it receives an immediate result. As soon as she touches the garment of the sinless Son of God, "the flow of blood [dries] up, and she [feels] in her body that she [is] healed of her disease" (Mark 5:29).

Jesus perceives "in himself that power [has] gone out from him" and asks, "Who touched my garments?" (v. 30). The disciples think this is a ridiculous question since "the crowd" is "pressing around" (v. 31). But Jesus "can always distinguish between the jostle of a curious mob, and the agonized touch of a needy soul."[1] Jesus wants to do more than take away this woman's illness. He also wants to take away her shame and restore her to real community. By stopping, turning, and publicly declaring, "Your faith has made you well" (v. 34), Jesus heals her in more ways than one.

As Jesus and the others approach Jairus's home, they discover that his daughter is now dead. "Do not fear, only believe," Jesus says (v. 36). If Jesus could heal his daughter before she died, then he can raise her from the dead as well. When Jesus is involved, his will is done no matter what. He puts all the scoffers outside "and [takes] the child's father and mother" to where the girl lies (v. 40).

In both cases, Jesus spoke tender, life-giving words. "Daughter, your faith has made you well," he tells the twelve-year outcast (v. 34). "Little girl, I say to you, arise," he tells the dead twelve-year-old girl (v. 41). "And immediately the girl got up and began walking" and he "told them to give her something to eat" (vv. 42–43). Jesus, the Great Physician, cares for the whole person, both body and soul.

Like the religious leader and his wife, we are helpless. We are powerless to heal ourselves or raise our loved ones from the dead. Like the outcast woman, we are broken and bankrupt without Christ. But, in Jesus, we have a sure hope. One day the angel will blow the trumpet, Jesus will command us to arise, and we will be fully whole in the presence of our Savior.

TALK TO YOURSELF. Do you sometimes feel hopeless and helpless or think that your trial will never end? Remember, Jesus delights to help the helpless.

1. G. Campbell Morgan, *The Gospel According to Mark* (New York: Fleming H. Revell, 1927), 128.

TALK TO GOD. Take one of your current heartaches or body aches to the Lord. Ask him to use the pain to draw you closer to Jesus.

TALK TO OTHERS. Think about one of your friends, a family member, or a brother or sister in church who is struggling with ongoing pain or sickness. Consider reading this meditation to them and praying with them.

68. A New Body

For we know that if the tent that is our earthly home is destroyed, we have a building from God, a house not made with hands, eternal in the heavens. (2 Cor. 5:1)

Pain always involves our bodies. It can be no other way. We feel even intellectual and emotional suffering in the body, whether there is a cause-and-effect relationship that makes sense to us. This is because we are embodied spirits—we are each made of a body and soul . . . together . . . always.

When we suffer, it's helpful for us to remember that the bodies we currently inhabit are temporary. Someday, at the resurrection, we will get new ones—bodies that are immune to suffering of any kind. Until then, "we groan" under varied burdens, while "longing to put on our heavenly dwelling" (2 Cor. 5:2).

Today's verse encourages us to be confident in our knowledge that even "if the tent that is our earthly home is destroyed, we have a building from God, a house not made with hands, eternal in the heavens." Though the bodies we now occupy are built by God, we have another building from God that is infinitely better: an eternal home with him. Our current flesh and blood "cannot inherit the kingdom of God, nor does the perishable inherit the imperishable" (1 Cor. 15:50), but one day all who know Jesus will be raised to receive new bodies that will live in everlasting glory with the Savior. When that day comes, your perishable body will put on the imperishable, and your mortal body will put on immortality (see v. 53). This resurrected body will be the eternal house for your soul, and the new heavens and earth will be your eternal home.

Even now Jesus is preparing that place for those who trust in him. Before he ascended bodily into heaven, he spoke these reassuring words to his followers: "In my Father's house are many rooms. If it were not so, would I have told you that I go to prepare a place for you? And if I go and prepare a place for you, I will come again and will take you to myself, that where I am you may be also" (John 14:2–3). The disciples were rightly troubled. Jesus had just told them he was going to leave them. He was now aiming the rest of his life straight at the cross. But he helped them to put trouble in its proper place by redirecting their attention to their promised future. In a world filled with trouble and all kinds of suffering, what a comfort it is to have Jesus as our refuge and heaven as our eternal resting place!

Suffering is in us and all around us, but if we are trusting in Jesus as our Savior and Lord, we have a sure promise. One day, our spirits will be delivered from our bodies of disease, disability, and death, and we will be clothed with an eternal tent—a building that is better than our current house. Therefore, "we are always of good courage. We know that while we are at home in the body we are away from the Lord, for we walk by faith, not by sight" (2 Cor. 5:6–7).

TALK TO YOURSELF. Do you have a balanced view of your earthly body? Do you see it as a temporary dwelling place? How might you know if you are caring for your body with proper stewardship without idolizing your health or physique?

TALK TO GOD. Journal a prayer that expresses thanks for the promise of the future resurrection that will usher in your receiving a new, glorified body.

TALK TO OTHERS. Ask a mature Christian to share with you some ways God has used suffering to wean their affection away from the world and turn the eyes of their heart to eternity.

69. Take Your Troubles to the Lord

The LORD makes poor and makes rich; he brings low and
he exalts. He raises up the poor from the dust; he lifts the
needy from the ash heap to make them sit with princes and
inherit a seat of honor. For the pillars of the earth are the
LORD's, and on them he has set the world. (1 Sam. 2:7–8)

In college, I enjoyed learning how to develop film in a darkroom. My classmates and I had to be very careful to never turn on the light or open the door without permission from the person inside. If the film was not in complete darkness long enough, it would not develop.

Faith is like that; it develops in the dark times. Our trust in the Lord is tested when we cannot comprehend our circumstances but still wonder what God might be doing behind the scenes. It was this way for an Old Testament woman who lived in the stormy days of the judges. The tedious repetition of the five-step cycle of rest, rebellion, retribution, repentance, and restoration was finally ending, and the time of the kings was on the horizon.

As the war-torn drama unfolds, the camera lens zooms in on a heartbreaking scene. Lonely and rejected, Hannah finds herself tormented internally, by the shame of her barrenness, and externally, by aggravation and verbal abuse from her rival wife. Hannah's humble response to her trial and her heartfelt trust in her sovereign Lord reveal three lessons that help us in puzzling times.

Rest in God when life hurts and your expectations are unmet. Hannah's marriage was less than ideal. As one of two women married to the same man, she was his, but he was not hers. Elkanah was a man of position in society, the kind of man who needs an heir. But Hannah, his first wife, was barren; "The Lord had closed her womb" (1 Sam. 1:5). So, caving into cultural pressure, Elkanah took a second wife.

Hannah's name means *grace*, while her rival's, Peninnah, means *pearl*. But Peninnah wasn't a pearl. She was a pain. One commentator calls her "an overly fertile, mouthy, thorn in the flesh."[2] She made Hannah's life so miserable that Hannah "wept and would not eat" (1 Sam. 1:7). Deeply distressed, Hannah "prayed to the Lord and wept bitterly" (v. 10). When your life hurts and your expectations fail, do you rest in the Lord?

Run to God in prayer, surrendering your deepest desires. Hannah's affliction accomplished what suffering is so often sent to do: It drove her to prayer. It pushed her to a place of unprecedented surrender to God. Her pain broke her will. And in her brokenness, Hannah learned to run to the best place—to God. She laid out her

---

2. Dale Ralph Davis, *1 Samuel: Looking on the Heart,* rev. ed. (Fearn: Christian Focus, 2010), 15.

heart's desire—a son—and made a vow to "give him to the LORD all the days of his life" (1 Sam. 1:11). Three times Hannah referred to herself as God's *servant*. With that humble mindset, she was ready not only to receive a son from God but also to release him to the Lord's service after she weaned him (see vv. 19–28). Even before he was conceived, Hannah was preparing to let go of her son. Have you surrendered your deepest desire to God?

Resolve to praise God and trust his sovereign plan. Hannah kept her vow by giving her son back to the Lord. And when she did, her heart burst: "My heart exults in the LORD; my horn is exalted in the LORD" (1 Sam. 2:1). Hannah's prayer richly recognized God's sovereignty over her trials and his ability to answer prayer. "There is none holy like the LORD . . . there is no rock like our God" (v. 2). The LORD "brings low and he exalts . . . he lifts the needy from the ash heap. . . . For the pillars of the earth are the LORD's, and on them he has set the world." Hannah's faith was fueled by confidence in her sovereign Lord. She trusted her Creator, the one who upholds the whole world, including hers. What more solid foundation could anyone build upon?

TALK TO YOURSELF. Is there an unmet desire that nags at your heart? What is it?

TALK TO GOD. Pray through Hannah's prayer in 1 Samuel 2:1–10, applying it to your situation.

TALK TO OTHERS. Is there a couple in your church who is walking through the trial of infertility? How might you encourage them this week?

70. Take Joy in the God of Your Salvation

Though the fig tree should not blossom, nor fruit be on the vines, the produce of the olive fail and the fields yield no food, the flock be cut off from the fold and there be no herd in the stalls, yet I will rejoice in the LORD; I will take joy in the God of my salvation. GOD, the Lord, is my strength; he makes my feet like the deer's; he makes me tread on my high places.
(Hab. 3:17–19)

Years ago, my sister drew my attention to a Scripture passage that I had not noticed before. My wife and I were struggling to make ends meet for our large and growing family. Our worn-out van had more than two hundred thousand miles on it, and we had no means of replacing it. In my mind's eye, I can still see where I was standing in the church parsonage when my sister called and read today's verses to me. Since then, I have come to see them as some of the most beautiful verses in the entire Bible. During seasons of suffering, they've been the lifeblood of my soul.

Perhaps these closing lines of the prophet's song have become yours too. If not, I hope they grow on you, beginning today. Read them again—this time slower.

Habakkuk, the book's namesake, is a frustrated and confused prophet whose name means *embrace* or *wrestle*. Even as he embraced God's calling, Habakkuk wrestled first with why a holy God would seem to tolerate wickedness in Judah, then why God would employ an even more wicked nation to chastise his people. In Habakkuk 1, he voices his agonizing "How long?" questions to God. God answers him by essentially saying, "I'm working behind the scenes. Trust me." Finally, God's prophet is humbled, ready to listen and trust, and he bursts forth in praise.

Habakkuk 3 is a musical prayer with one simple message: *God is fully trustworthy and unlimited in power and is, therefore, our only hope.* It's an example of how "the righteous shall live by his faith" (2:4), especially when we don't understand God's ways. In Habakkuk 3, we see two actions that proceed from God-centered faith.

Recount the saving works of the Lord. Reports of the mighty works of Yahweh fill the prophet's heart with awe: "Your work, O LORD, do I fear" (3:2) Yet the works of God in the past also bring him hope in the here and now. He pleads with God to "revive" his work among his people as the time for judgment draws near (v. 2). God's glory flows from him—like the rays of the sun—as pestilence, plagues, and all nature bow to his sovereignty and express his wrath against the wicked (vv. 3–12). Still, God goes "out for the salvation of [his] people" (v. 13; see also vv. 14–15). When disturbed by life's troubles, recount the mighty deeds of the Lord. Look to him for rescue and the judgment of your enemies. God's timing is almost always slower than yours would be, but it's never late. Rest in him.

Rejoice in the Lord, not in circumstances. When life feels like a fig tree that doesn't blossom, or an olive grove that fails to produce fruit, set your sights on the Lord. Like Habakkuk, say with a determined heart, "Yet I will rejoice in the LORD" (v. 18). Learn to root your joy in the grace of God. Say, "I will take joy in the God of my salvation" (v. 18). Then, no matter what life throws your way, you will be able to bound up rocky terrain with "feet like the deer's" (v. 19) Why? Because "GOD, the Lord, is [your] strength" (v. 19).

Perhaps Habakkuk's famine and drought illustrate your current financial situation, marriage, employment, or health, or something else. Take heart. No matter what your suffering looks or feels like, the beauty of biblical truths like these will refresh your weary soul when you make a choice to rejoice.

TALK TO YOURSELF. Can you think of a season in your life when you felt fruitless and without hope? Do you remember a time when God disciplined you, yet he did so with mercy? What have you learned from such times?

TALK TO GOD. Pray through Habakkuk 3:17–19 with your personal "drought" or "famine" in mind.

TALK TO OTHERS. Write a note of encouragement to a brother or sister in your church who is in a difficult season of life. Use today's Scripture to give them hope.

SPIRITUAL DISCERNMENT

71. When Suffering Is Nobody's Fault

As he passed by, he saw a man blind from birth. And his disciples asked him, "Rabbi, who sinned, this man or his parents, that he was born blind?" Jesus answered, "It was not that this man sinned, or his parents, but that the works of God might be displayed in him." (John 9:1–3)

Eighteen years ago, my wife and I were standing in the kitchen of the old farmhouse we planned to renovate. She said, with tears streaming down her face, "What did I do wrong? Was it something I ate during my pregnancy? Or was it something I failed to eat? Is God punishing our daughter for something I've done? Am I the reason our precious little Kayte was born deaf?"

As I held my wife, her heart did not agonize alone. I was also asking questions, though only inwardly: "Lord, I've given my whole life to your service and been willing to sacrifice everything earthly. Is that not good enough? What more must I do to earn your favor? Is it my fault our daughter is cognitively disabled? Are you angry at me?"

Let me be clear. My wife and I would never choose a different life. We are grateful to the Lord for creating four of our ten children with hearing impairments. It's now hard for us to imagine life without the blessings of disability. But as we've walked this journey for more than three decades, there have been times when, in our weakness, we've struggled with doubts like anyone else. Perhaps you've asked similar questions in the face of your suffering.[1]

When unexpected trials arrive on your doorstep, you may be tempted to blame someone—that is, to make a direct connection between specific wrongdoing and specific consequences. The disciples certainly succumbed to that temptation. "Rabbi, who sinned, this man or his parents, that he was born blind?" The Bible does teach that there are consequences to sin and that all of life's griefs trickle down from mankind's original sin (see Gen. 3:14–19). However, there is not always a direct cause-and-effect relationship between specific affliction and specific sin. Jesus makes this clear.

The disciples were more concerned about figuring out whose sin caused this man's disability than they were with learning how to minister with compassion. To the disciples, the blind man was a problem to be solved. To Jesus, he was a person to be loved. But Jesus surprises them when he reveals a higher purpose. The disability wasn't the blind man's fault or the fault of his parents: he was blind by God's design. It was so "that the works of God might be displayed in him." Clearly, the governing force behind the suffering this man and his parents endured was not any one person's sin but God's larger agenda to display his powerful work and the glory of his grace. This man was born blind on purpose— that is, according to the purposes of God. We must not miss this!

When Jesus opens the blind man's eyes, the physical healing isn't the most important part of the story. Jesus goes beyond

---

1. I explore this and related themes in depth with Joni Eareckson Tada in our book, *When Disability Hits Home: How God Magnifies His Grace in Our Weakness and Suffering* (Wapwallopen, PA: Shepherd Press, 2020).

opening his physical eyes; he opens his spiritual eyes as well. The blind man becomes a Christ-follower; he is saved. Jesus healed his greatest disability: the blindness of his heart (see John 9:35–37).

God's ways are higher than our ways (see Isa. 55:9). Rarely do we recognize his purpose for our suffering. But, at a minimum, we know this: Suffering is a God-ordained means of displaying his wisdom and power. It's his way of shifting our earthbound focus from temporal comforts to what is infinitely more valuable in light of eternity—knowing Jesus.

TALK TO YOURSELF. Why do you think the default human response to suffering is to pin the blame on ourselves or someone else? Do you ever respond this way? If so, what does your response reveal about your view of God's character and providence?

TALK TO GOD. Pray through Psalm 16.

TALK TO OTHERS. Make a "Works of God" page or two in your journal. Begin recounting the works of the Lord that you see in your life because of suffering. Share a few of these with a friend in Christ.

72. When Suffering Is Your Fault

*You have dealt with me because of all my transgressions; for
my groans are many, and my heart is faint. (Lam. 1:22)*

Suffering that is nobody's fault may be hard to accept. Perhaps
more difficult, though, are painful situations that we bring upon
ourselves. When we realize what we've done, repent, and confess
our foolishness to God, we may be tempted to wonder if he has
really forgiven us. *If God has forgiven me, why am I still suffering
the consequences?*

But God loves us enough to let us reap what we sow in order
that we may humble ourselves and receive more abundant grace
(see James 4:6). In times of regret, it's important to remember
that the Lord's mercy abounds and his grace is greater than all our
sin. This is one big lesson we can glean from today's verse and its
surroundings.

Jeremiah wrote Lamentations after Jerusalem was destroyed
by God's enemies. "Judah has gone into exile," and "her pursuers
have all overtaken her" (Lam. 1:3). The "roads . . . mourn" and
"her priests" and "all her people groan" (vv. 4, 11). We may imagine the prophet looking over the wreckage as he remembers the
glory of her former days. "How lonely sits the city that was full of
people!" (v. 1).

The cause of Jeremiah's deepest sorrow, however, is his real-
ization that Judah herself is to blame for what has happened:
"Jerusalem sinned grievously" (1:8), and the Lord has afflicted
her "for the multitude of her transgressions" (v. 5). God's city is
personified as a woman who testifies, "The LORD is in the right,
for I have rebelled against his word" (v. 18) and then prays, "My
heart is wrung within me, because I have been very rebellious. . . .
You have dealt with me because of all my transgressions" (vv. 20,
22). Her deep-seated rebellion, pride, and stubbornness caused

her ruin. Now all blame-shifting is gone. Her true brokenness over her sin leads to repentance.

Jeremiah shows that we can remember the mercy of God even when we are the cause of our pain. He chooses to "call to mind" the "steadfast love of the Lord," which, in turn, enables him to say from the heart, "Therefore I have hope" (3:21–22). "The steadfast love of the Lord" is sometimes translated "the Lord's lovingkindnesses" (NASB), from the plural form of the Hebrew word *chesed*. In the Old Testament, it's the closest equivalent to the New Testament concept of grace.

When Jeremiah refers to God's "mercies," he uses a word related to the Hebrew word for *womb* that communicates tender care and affection. Yahweh's grace and tender care "never come to an end; they are new every morning" (3:22–23). Not "new" in the sense that they never existed before but "new" in the sense that they are refreshed each day. The same God who loved you yesterday loves you today. And when you got out of bed this morning, he stood ready to supply you with all the mercy you will need.

When we have brought trouble on ourselves, we may be tempted to get stuck in grief or grow bitter over the ways that sin has tricked us and stolen from us. But heartfelt repentance is more profitable than self-loathing. When God employs the effects of our sin to chasten us, it is because he wishes to restore us.

The prophet Hosea encapsulates this truth in his call to rebellious Israel: "Come, let us return to the Lord; for he has torn us, that he may heal us; he has struck us down, and he will bind us up (Hos. 6:1). If we humble ourselves before God, saying, "This is my doing. God is chastening me. I am the one who brought this misery upon myself," only then are we ready to receive his mercy.

Deep hope is born out of the depths of repentance. The humility that leads to repentance also leads to restoration. This, in turn, leads to newfound hope. "'The Lord is my portion,' says my soul, 'therefore I will hope in him'" (Lam. 3:24).

TALK TO YOURSELF. Do you live with regrets or painful consequences of your sin? If so, it's appropriate to chronicle your pain and recount from where you have fallen. Just don't dwell there. List ways in which you turned away from the Lord and describe how he used pain to bring you back. Then read Proverbs 16:16–19 and rewrite all the "better" sayings in your own words. For example, "How much better it is for *me* to acquire wisdom than gold" (v. 16).

TALK TO GOD. Personified as a grieving woman, the devastated city of Zion acknowledges, "The LORD is in the right, for I have rebelled against his word" (Lam. 1:18). Write a similar prayer that acknowledges how right it is for God to chasten you when you stray from him.

TALK TO OTHERS. Is someone you know suffering under the weight of the heartbreaking consequences of their own choices? Read Galatians 6:1–5, and prayerfully consider how you might minister grace to them in gentleness and humility. Perhaps consider sharing the gist of this day's reading to encourage them. If the Spirit leads you to have this restorative ministry in their life, be sure to prayerfully evaluate your own life in the light of Jesus's admonition in Matthew 7:1–5.

73. Suffering Is Your Teacher

Teach me good judgment and knowledge, for I believe in your commandments. Before I was afflicted I went astray, but now I keep your word. (Ps. 119:66–67)

Mrs. Schmidt was my favorite childhood teacher. Not only did she get me interested in reading books, but she was also a cute brunette. Yes, I had a crush on my third-grade teacher! Most important of all, however, her heartfelt love and concern were cemented in my memory the morning she called me to her desk. "Are you OK?" she asked.

The evening before, my mom, two of my brothers, and I had been in a car accident that should have killed at least one of us. My brothers and I were released from the hospital the same evening, but Mom remained for six weeks because of a shattered left arm and hip. While she was in the hospital, neighbors brought over numerous casseroles and other meals to feed our hard-working dad and his six children. The kindness of my teacher and our neighbors made a lasting impression on me. Suffering can do the same for us. It can be both a teacher and a friend.

Today's verses flow from the heart of a man who reaped at least some of the benefits of suffering. His suffering did not leave him bitter. Instead, he prayed, "Teach me good judgment and knowledge, for I believe in your commandments." When he had gone astray, God had faithfully sent affliction to help him to discern what was good and to motivate him to return to the path of obedience. Instead of being angry at God, he prayed, "You have dealt well with your servant" (Ps. 119:65). The psalmist's post-trial exclamation is worthy of our attention: "It is good for me that I was afflicted, that I might learn your statutes" (v. 71). Affliction tenderized his heart, making it more receptive to biblical instruction. He learned from the error of his ways.

Suffering is a faithful teacher. This is a recurring theme in Scripture. Consider more of the benefits of affliction:[2]

- Suffering teaches us to be aware of the power of God, to whom we owe our sustenance (see Ps. 68:19).
- Suffering teaches us humility (see 2 Cor. 12:7).
- Suffering teaches us that God is concerned more about character than comfort (see Rom. 5:3–4; Heb. 12:10–11).
- Suffering teaches us that the greatest good of the Christian life is not the absence of pain but Christlikeness (see Rom. 8:28–29; 2 Cor. 4:8–10).
- Suffering teaches us obedience and self-control (see Ps. 119:67; Rom. 5:1–5; Heb. 5:8; James 1:2–8).
- Suffering teaches us to number our days so that we present to God a heart of wisdom (see Ps. 90:7–12).
- Suffering teaches us how to comfort others when they suffer (see 2 Cor. 1:3–11).
- Suffering teaches us to remember that Christ is our highest treasure (see Phil. 3:8).
- Suffering teaches us to leave injustices with God, who is the ultimate Judge (see Ps. 58:10–11).
- Suffering teaches us to give thanks in times of sorrow (see 1 Thess. 5:18; 2 Cor. 1:11).

Suffering is an essential piece in the Christian living curriculum. In the hands of our wise and good heavenly Father, it serves us well when we listen to its lessons.

2. These examples are adapted from one of my favorite books on suffering, written by Joni Eareckson Tada and Steven Estes, *When God Weeps: Why Our Sufferings Matter to the Almighty* (Grand Rapids: Zondervan, 2000), 232–40.

TALK TO YOURSELF. Can you say with the psalmist, "It is good for me that I was afflicted"? In your journal, list some of the ways that suffering has trained you to walk in God's ways more consistently.

TALK TO GOD. At the end of your list, write a prayer of thanksgiving.

TALK TO OTHERS. Get together with a fellow Christian. Read Psalm 119:65–72 together and talk about the benefits of suffering you both have experienced. Then pray through the passage together.

74. Benefits of Pruning

By this my Father is glorified, that you bear much fruit and so prove to be my disciples. (John 15:8)

Like an oddly shaped tree with dead branches or suckers (small shoots) growing out of its trunk, we need pruning. We have sinful character qualities and deficiencies that God wants us to address. Corrupt desires feed our sinful behavior, sometimes leading to habits or addictions that we need to repent of and put off. In John 15:1–8, Jesus mentions five benefits of God's pruning.

God prunes you so that you will bear more fruit. God does not prune his redeemed children because he is angry at them, nor does he prune them because Jesus's sacrifice was not enough (perish the thought!). God prunes his branches so "that [you] may bear more fruit" (15:2). God looks at your Christian life and concludes that you are not bearing as much fruit as you could be. You are out of balance and have sickly leaves, dead branches, and suckers draining away your spiritual vitality. These hindrances need to be removed.

God prunes you so that you will become more dependent. God prunes you so that you will learn to abide in Christ—the true source of your life. To abide in Christ means to live in obedient dependence on his ongoing, minute-by-minute supply of grace—grace that flows from him. Too often we become proud and independent, functioning as practical atheists. But this will never lead to greater fruitfulness. "Abide in me, and I in you. As the branch cannot bear fruit by itself, unless it abides in the vine, neither can you, unless you abide in me" (15:4). Your Father, the vinedresser, trains you to learn—in practice, not only in precept—that you truly "can do nothing" apart from union with Christ (v. 5).

God prunes you to assure you of your salvation. God does not prune unbelievers so that they may become more fruitful, because their fruits would consist of more dead works (see Heb. 9:14; James 2:17). Eventually, they will be "thrown into the fire, and burned" (John 15:6). The painful pruning of your character does not undermine the Spirit's work of assurance; it strengthens it. The true child of God is chastened by the heavenly Father. The illegitimate child is not (see Heb. 12:7–8). By your fruitfulness, you "prove to be" a genuine follower of Christ.

God prunes you so that he is free to answer more of your prayers. Submission to divine pruning results in your learning to abide in Christ, which in turn results in the freedom to ask God "whatever you wish, and it will be done for you" (John 15:7). God built the "obedience connection" into prayer to motivate you to continue to walk by faith. It is one of the if/then relationships in the Christian life.

God prunes you so that you will glorify him. Jesus is crystal clear: "By this my Father is glorified, that you bear much fruit." To *glorify* means to draw attention to something. As a believer in Christ, you should live to draw attention not to yourself but to your God and Savior. Your redemption brings God glory in order that the world may know that the gospel is real (see, for example, 1 Thess. 1:2–8).

God prunes those whom he loves—those who truly belong to him as blood-bought children. The heavenly Vinedresser trims wherever is needed to shape us into the image of the true Vine, Jesus Christ. This happens as we learn to abide in him. Remember the words of Jesus: "I am the vine; you are the branches. Whoever abides in me and I in him, he it is that bears much fruit, for apart from me you can do nothing" (John 15:5).

TALK TO YOURSELF. How much fruit do you want your Christian life to bear? If your heart's longing is "much more fruit," then be prepared for the pruning that may be required.

TALK TO GOD. Ask God to cultivate humility in you so that you respond to his pruning with a willing heart.

TALK TO OTHERS. Do you know any believers who exemplify calm trust in the Lord during suffering? Tell them how their example helps your faith to grow.

75. Calling for Your Elders

Is anyone among you sick? Let him call for the elders of the church, and let them pray over him, anointing him with oil in the name of the Lord. (James 5:14)

James 5:13–18 is often neglected or misunderstood. Take a moment to open your Bible and read it. Every verse in the paragraph contains an explicit reference to prayer. Prayer, however, is not a discipline that James merely taught. He lived it. According to church history, he spent so much time in prayer that his knees became as calloused as those of a camel.[3] In today's reading, "Old Camel-Knees" makes it clear that one of the ways we trust God in times of suffering is by calling our church shepherds to pray with us and for us.

Following quick-fire exhortations to the suffering to pray, and to the cheerful to sing (see 5:13), James instructs the sick to "call for the elders of the church" to come to their home, or hospital, to pray. The word *sick* refers to bodily weakness but may denote any kind of weakness, whether mental, moral, or spiritual. James places the initiative on the sick person themselves to "call"—if possible. "Pray" is the central verb, the specific activity of the elders, while "anointing" is an activity secondary to praying. The oil is probably simple olive oil, an oil commonly used to honor guests. In this context, the oil probably symbolizes the presence of the Spirit and the healing power of God. James does not regard the oil itself as a healing agent or the anointing as possessing magical power; it is "the prayer of faith" that heals (v. 15).

The prayer of faith produces three results. First, the troubled believer may be restored, which may include physical healing, if

---

3. Matt Erickson, "Old Camel Knees: A Brief Reflection on the Remarkable Prayer Life of James the Just," *Renovate* (blog), August 29, 2019, https://mwerickson.com/2019/08/29/old-camel-knees-a-brief-reflection-on-the-remarkable-prayer-life-of-james-the-just/.

God wills: "And the prayer of faith will save the one who is sick, and the Lord will raise him up" (5:15). Second, if spiritual healing is necessary, God will use physical pain to lead the sufferer to confess their sin with a broken spirit. As a result, their sins "will be forgiven" (v. 15). Third, if the sickness is the result of sin, which is not always the case (see John 9:1–3), repentance will yield practical righteousness. The "righteous person" (James 5:16) is not someone who never sins but someone who, when they sin, humbly deals with their offense. When this kind of person offers the prayer of faith, it "has great power" (v. 16).

Suffering should always drive us to pray for ourselves, but at times it should also compel us to reach out to our church shepherds. Prayer ministry is a gracious provision from the Lord in times of sickness and pain and one of the beautiful features of God's design for his church.

TALK TO YOURSELF. J. C. Ryle wrote, "We should cultivate the habit of expecting answers to our prayers. We should do like the merchant who sends his ships to sea. We should not be satisfied, unless we see some return."[4] When you pray, do you have the expectation of the merchant? Why or why not?

TALK TO GOD. Read Psalm 66:18. Do you have any unconfessed sin that you need to talk to the Lord about?

TALK TO OTHERS. Are you sick? Why not call the elders of your church and ask them to come to minister the Word and pray with you?

4. John Charles Ryle, "Prayer," in *Practical Religion: New and Revised Edition* (London: 1900), 91. Available online as "A Call to Prayer" at https://www .monergism.com/call-prayer.

ANCHOR YOUR FAITH TO GOD'S PROMISES

76. Jesus Will Never Leave You Alone

Keep your life free from love of money, and be content with what you have, for he has said, "I will never leave you nor forsake you." So we can confidently say, "The Lord is my helper; I will not fear; what can man do to me?" (Heb. 13:5–6)

When we suffer, nothing is more important than knowing that we are not alone. That is why God has strengthened his people by reminding them of his active presence. For example, when God called Joshua to lead his people into the promised land, he assured him, "The LORD your God is with you wherever you go" (Josh. 1:9). Or consider these age-old promises delivered by Isaiah:

> When you pass through the waters, I will be with you;
>   and through the rivers, they shall not overwhelm you;
> when you walk through fire you shall not be burned,
>   and the flame shall not consume you. (Isa. 43:2)

From of old no one has heard
  or perceived by the ear,
no eye has seen a God besides you,
    who acts for those who wait for him. (64:4)

Though we cannot see what God is doing behind the scenes, we may rest in knowing that he is working on our behalf—for our good and his glory—and we may be confident that he is with us. Our awareness of God's presence is not determined by our emotions but comes as we embrace scriptural promises by faith.

These promises, and the lessons learned by God's Old Testament people, are meant to bring great comfort to you too: "Now these things happened to them as an example, but they were written down for our instruction, on whom the end of the ages has come" (1 Cor. 10:11). Even though these promises were given first to God's covenant nation, Israel, they contain truths that transcend time and can therefore be claimed by believers in Jesus: "For all the promises of God find their Yes in him" (2 Cor. 1:20). This is where it gets personal for you and me.

The Son of God became Immanuel, God with us (see Isa. 7:14; Matt. 1:23). He broke into history to save us from our sins and give us new life. In Christ, God is on our side. And if God is for us, then ultimately no one can be against us (see Rom. 8:31). When you are tempted to think you are alone, remember that Jesus says to you, "I will never leave you nor forsake you." Jesus remains present by the Spirit whom he sent. Jesus is with you. He is right by your side. He is never far away but always present and attentive to all your ways and needs. You are never alone.

When we anchor our faith to God's promises, we are then able to say, "The Lord is my helper; I will not fear."

TALK TO YOURSELF. Like the writer of Hebrews, remind yourself of this reality: "The Lord is my helper; I will not fear; what can man do to me?"

TALK TO GOD. His promised presence produces contentment in your heart despite difficult circumstances. Do you see any discontent in your heart? Talk to God about it. Ask for his forgiveness where needed. And ask for help to trust him more.

TALK TO OTHERS. Whom do you know who is suffering right now and might feel alone? Consider sharing today's Scripture with them or arranging a time to meet up with them.

77. Consider Jesus

My God, my God, why have you forsaken me? Why are you so far from saving me, from the words of my groaning? O my God, I cry by day, but you do not answer, and by night, but I find no rest. (Ps. 22:1–2)

Suffering comes into our lives through various channels. Most troubling is when evils are willfully committed against us by other people. Mistreatment damages the human soul in ways that only the God of redemption may fully heal. Therefore, when we have been exploited or harmed by others, or when we are given the opportunity to minister grace to others who have been harmed, our deepest need is to reflect on the One who was mistreated more than any other. The soul of the abused or oppressed person always requires care.

We need the inner peace, security, and healing that flow from Jesus, the Lover of our souls. He not only knows all about our past and present suffering but also genuinely empathizes with us. Our broken and disillusioned spirits receive their ultimate comfort and counsel from the One who loves us more than any other; however, this level of care and empathy came at great expense. Jesus endured the ultimate abandonment to secure our safe standing before God and relationship with our heavenly Father.

Consider the sufferings of Jesus. Psalm 22 is one of the greatest testimonies to the integrity of Scripture. Only the Holy Spirit could have accurately recorded David's real-life experiences in such a way that they also perfectly foreshadowed our Savior's suffering. In this psalm, the troubles and abuses of our Savior, David's greater Son, are thoroughly described.

- He felt a deep sense of abandonment from loss of relationship (vv. 1–2). Compare these verses with Mark 15:33–34.
- He was despised by others (v. 6). Meditate on Isaiah 53:3.
- He endured looks of contempt and mocking gestures (v. 7). Read Mark 15:27–30.
- He was verbally assaulted (v. 8). See this fulfilled in Mark 15:31–32 and Luke 23:39.
- He felt alone and in trouble (v. 11). For one example, read Matthew 26:38–40.
- He was surrounded by enemies (vv. 12–13). Compare Mark 15:6–15.
- He was crushed in spirit and physically exhausted to the point of death (vv. 14–15). Meditate on John 19:28–30.
- He endured intense pain (v. 16). John 19:1–3 describes some, as does Luke 23:33.
- He was publicly humiliated (v. 17). For one example, read Luke 23:35.

- He felt the shame of nakedness (v. 18). See the fulfillment of this in Matthew 27:28, 35.
- He needed outside help (vv. 19–21). Read Mark 14:35–36; 15:20–21.

Let me be clear. The mistreatment that Jesus endured was unique; it was *unlike* ours in that it was the appointed atonement that God required. However, his suffering is *like* ours in such a way that he can understand and be our empathetic High Priest. Pondering the myriad ways that he suffered knits our hearts more tightly to his and helps us to grow in compassion and empathy toward others.

Consider the strength and sympathy of God. Mingled throughout the horrific suffering described in Psalm 22 are truths about the character of God, who is the ultimate source of your strength. God is holy and sovereign (v. 3), trustworthy (v. 4), dependable (v. 5), near to those in trouble (vv. 9–10), and our helper (vv. 19–21). It's also vital for you to remember God's tender attention to "the affliction of the afflicted" (v. 24).

Nestled in King David's cries for help and his bold declarations of faith are tender reminders of our Lord's compassion. Out of the depths of David's suffering emerges a stunning portrait of the most gracious counselor and caregiver, Jesus.

TALK TO YOURSELF. Read Hebrews 2:14–18. Why do you think these verses are immediately followed by the exhortation to "consider Jesus" (3:1)?

TALK TO GOD. Write a prayer of thanksgiving for the Savior's empathy for you in times of mistreatment.

TALK TO OTHERS. Do you know anyone who has experienced mistreatment or abuse? How does Psalm 22 inform the questions you should ask this person? Walk through this psalm with a fellow believer and look at how it is fulfilled in the gospel references in the bullet-point list.

78. They Reach the Shell, Not the Kernel

Some were tortured, refusing to accept release, so that they might rise again to a better life. Others suffered mocking and flogging, and even chains and imprisonment. They were stoned, they were sawn in two, they were killed with the sword. (Heb. 11:35–37)

What then shall we say to these things? If God is for us, who can be against us? (Rom. 8:31)

Church history records the extent to which the first disciples of Jesus suffered for their faith. Thomas Brooks, a 1600s British preacher, pinpointed this when he wrote, "All these precious servants of God, except John, died violent deaths, and so through sufferings entered into glory."[1] As they left this world, perhaps they remembered the words of Jesus, their Master: "'A servant is not greater than his master.' If they persecuted me, they will also persecute you" (John 15:20).

The author of Hebrews adds the enduring testimony of others. Some heroes of the faith "were tortured . . . suffered mocking and

---

1. Thomas Brooks, "Are We Mad Now to Pursue after Holiness?" reprinted in *Free Grace Broadcaster* 185 (Fall 2003): 32.

flogging . . . were stoned . . . were sawn in two" before being killed. Such mistreatment may be difficult for us to imagine if we have not experienced persecution, but suffering for the sake of Christ and the gospel is an honor bestowed on those who love God wholly. Paul warned young Timothy, "Indeed, all who desire to live a godly life in Christ Jesus will be persecuted" (2 Tim. 3:12). The pursuit of holiness may evoke fierce winds of opposition, but Thomas Brooks gives the following encouragement.

> All the troubles, afflictions, and persecutions that attend holiness can never reach a Christian's soul, they can never diminish a Christian's treasure; they reach the shell, not the kernel; the case, not the jewel; the lumber, not the goods; the [outbuilding], not the palace; the ribbon in the hat, not the gold in the purse. The most fiery trials and persecutions can never deprive a Christian of the special presence of God, nor of the light of his countenance, nor of the testimony of a good conscience, nor of the joys of the Spirit, nor of the pardon of sin, nor of fellowship with Christ, nor of the exercise of grace, nor of the hopes of glory.[2]

The apostle Paul embraced the same precious promises. Christ had spoken sobering words about him: "I will show [Paul] how much he must suffer for the sake of my name" (Acts 9:16). Nevertheless, Paul exalted the promise of everlasting life in the presence of God for all who are in Christ. "What then shall we say to these things? If God is for us, who can be against us?"

Throughout your life, you may face any number of unexpected trials that may threaten to steal what is most valuable to you. But these thieves can only rob you of temporal joys; they cannot

2. Brooks, 34.

reach your greatest treasure. Nothing—absolutely nothing—can ever cut you off "from the love of God in Christ Jesus our Lord" (Rom. 8:39).

TALK TO YOURSELF. Can you think of a time when enemies of Christ mistreated you? How did you respond? What kind of treatment do you expect from unbelievers, and why?

TALK TO GOD. Pray through Romans 8:31–39.

TALK TO OTHERS. Do you know someone who is suffering for righteousness' sake? Consider texting one or two of the promises in Romans 8:31–39 to them and let them know you are praying for the Spirit to strengthen their heart.

79. Joy Comes in the Morning

Weeping may last for the night, but a shout of joy comes in the morning. (Ps. 30:5 NASB)

Joy may be elusive at times. The trials of life threaten to engulf our joy like a thick fog moving over a lake. Many pressures have the potential of becoming joy robbers. Therefore, it's critical to remember these simple truths: Joy is the light of the living God that he infuses into us during the dark nights of the soul. It is the sturdy garment that clothes us after God turns our "mourning into dancing," and we lay aside the rough sackcloth of our grief to replace it "with gladness" (Ps. 30:11).

Psalm 30 is a song that has counseled my heart and restored my joy on more than one occasion. King David's transparency about his suffering is helpful. His joy was uprooted by relational conflict with his "foes," who rejoiced over his suffering (v. 1), and by illness that led to a close brush with death (see vv. 2–3). Yet David resolves to praise God amid his storm—"I will extol you, O Lord" (v. 1)—and invites other believers to join him: "Sing praises to the Lord, O you his saints" (v. 4). He compels all who will listen to accompany his praise, for two reasons.

God's acceptance lasts forever. God's anger is not long; it is "but for a moment" (Ps. 30:5). In vivid contrast, "his favor is for a lifetime" (v. 5). Loving-kindness is part of God's nature. Moses learned this on Mount Sinai when the Lord revealed his character: "The Lord, the Lord, a God merciful and gracious, slow to anger, and abounding in steadfast love and faithfulness" (Ex. 34:6). God does not display slow-burning irritation toward you even when you stray. That would be contrary to his nature.

But there's another reason, perhaps more important, that his anger is short. He already took out his wrath against your sin on Jesus, whom he "put forward as a propitiation by his blood" (Rom. 3:25). As a result, God's favor toward his blood-bought children will last forever.

Life's sorrows are temporary. Sadness is part of your experience as you walk with God in a broken world. But when you trust the Lord, you may be assured that your mourning is not permanent. It is only "for the night, but a shout of joy comes in the morning." Scripture assures you that just as the sunrise puts an end to night, so God will providentially restore your joy when your dark time of suffering comes to an end.

Like David, you can remind other believers of these truths. You can practice praising God along with others—even when your feelings may steer you away from praise. Together with others, you can sing to the Lord *while* you wait for your dark night to break forth in a sunrise of joy. "O LORD my God, I will give thanks to you forever!" (Ps. 30:12).

Sometimes in dark valleys we are tempted to hole up like wounded animals and privately lick our wounds. But we cannot endure times of hurt and sadness alone. In the church, God has given us a family of believers to walk through life with us. We can help one another to look to the Lord for the restoration of our joy.

TALK TO YOURSELF. What real or potential joy robbers do you see in your life? How do they threaten to overtake you?

TALK TO GOD. Pray through Psalm 30. Make it your own song of determined praise.

TALK TO OTHERS. Reach out to a mature believer. Ask if you can share your burden with them and if you can help to carry theirs. Resolve together to praise God amid your storms.

80. Being Trained in Righteousness

*For [our earthly fathers] disciplined us for a short time as it
seemed best to them, but he disciplines us for our good, that
we may share his holiness. For the moment all discipline
seems painful rather than pleasant, but later it yields the
peaceful fruit of righteousness to those who have been
trained by it. (Heb. 12:10–11)*

Since the basis of our justification is the righteousness of Christ—
not our own—our sin can no longer affect our standing before
God. We are fully accepted by God in Christ, and nothing can
ever change that. Because Jesus made peace with God through his
blood, the Father treats us not us as his enemies but as his beloved
children (see Eph. 2:14; Rom. 8:16–17). Forever, we are siblings
and friends of Jesus (see Heb. 2:11; John 15:15). Therefore, God
takes a long-range view of our relationship with him; he now treats
those who are in Christ "as sons" (Heb. 12:7).

So take heart. Your heavenly Father loves you too much to sit
back and do nothing when your sin threatens to harm you and
others. He "disciplines [you] for [your] good, that [you] may
share his holiness." Earthly fathers are flawed, and, though they
may discipline "for a short time as it [seems] best to them," their
correction is not always carried out with complete knowledge
or pure motives. But your heavenly Father's correction is always
good and properly administered because its goal is restorative—
never punitive. God does not punish his children—he disciplines
them. At first you may think this is a matter of semantics, but it's
an important distinction.

Punishment casts away, but discipline restores. Punishment
is for hardened subjects of wrath, but discipline is for beloved
children. Punishment requires payment for your sin, but discipline corrects you to protect you and bless you, *because* your sin

has already been paid for by Jesus. Punishment focuses on your past sins, but discipline, although addressing your disobedience, anticipates that your true repentance will lead to obedience and future blessing. Your past may include unwelcome consequences for your actions, as does mine, but you need not fear everlasting judgment, for "fear has to do with punishment" (1 John 4:18) and Jesus already endured yours. Now your heavenly Father demonstrates his ongoing love for you by training you to walk on his path so that you may yield "the peaceful fruit of righteousness."

Be encouraged! When you endure seasons of correction, though painful "for the moment," they are evidence of your Father's love, not his hatred. If God did not chasten you for choosing a pathway of sin, then you could not be assured that you were one of his blood-bought children (see Heb. 12:8). Therefore, do not be anxious about the Lord's correction in your life. On the contrary, be alarmed if you are living in disobedience without experiencing his chastening. God's discipline is proof of your adoption and a demonstration of his unending love for you.

TALK TO YOURSELF. How do you typically respond to God's correction?

TALK TO GOD. Write a prayer of praise to God for relating to you no longer as Judge but, now that you are in Christ, as your loving Father.

TALK TO OTHERS. Read Hebrews 12:3–11 with someone in your family or church. What truths about God bring you comfort? What truths encourage you to not grow fainthearted in your fight against remaining sin?

BENEFITS OF TRIALS

81. Obedience and Prayer

Whatever you ask in my name, this I will do, that the Father may be glorified in the Son. If you ask me anything in my name, I will do it. If you love me, you will keep my commandments. (John 14:13–15)

Paul Miller paints a thrilling picture of our privileged entry into God's throne room.

> Imagine that your prayer is a poorly dressed beggar reeking of alcohol and body odor, stumbling toward the palace of the great king. You have become your prayer. As you shuffle toward the barred gate, the guards stiffen. Your smell has preceded you. You stammer out a message for the great king: "I want to see the king." Your words are barely intelligible, but you whisper one final word, "Jesus. I come in the name of Jesus." At the name of Jesus, as if by magic, the palace comes alive. The guards snap to attention, bowing low in front of you. Lights come on, and the door flies open. You are ushered into the palace and down a long hallway into the throne room

of the great king, who comes running to you and wraps you in his arms.[1]

Such is the access we have to God because of our union with Jesus.

Now, imagine if you got whatever you prayed for whenever you asked for it without any conditions—even if you were rebelling against God or your life was characterized by unconfessed sin. You would be like a foolish child whose growth to maturity is hindered by their parents' indulgence. However, your heavenly Father knows how much sin harms his children; he doesn't pamper you, because he wants you to flourish. This explains why today's Scripture highlights the important cause-and-effect relationship between obedience and answered prayer.

Jesus promises to do whatever you ask "in [his] name"—that is, to do what is consistent with his character and will—so that the Father "may be glorified in the Son." However, in addition to encouraging you to take advantage of your free access to the throne of grace, Jesus connects the effectiveness of your prayer to your obedience when he says, "If you love me, you will keep my commandments." When you obey God's Word, it confirms that you love him and walk according to his name (see John 14:21–23; 15:14; 1 John 5:3). If you do not walk in obedience, then your professed love for Christ may be in question. At the very least, it is immature.

Parental love moves God to sometimes withhold his answer to our prayers in order to promote our increased loving obedience to him. "For this is the love of God, that we keep his commandments," writes John, but he also encourages us as he adds, "His commandments are not burdensome" (1 John 5:3). God's commands are not too hard for us to obey, because the indwelling Spirit energizes us to walk in the way of the Word.

---

1. Paul E. Miller, *A Praying Life: Connecting with God in a Distracting World* (Colorado Springs: NavPress, 2009), 135.

TALK TO YOURSELF. Read 1 John 3:21–23. What does it have to say about your positional righteousness (justification) and practical righteousness (obedience)? What does this mean for you?

TALK TO GOD. Read 1 John 1:5–10. Are you aware of any forms of disobedience, either of commission or of omission, that may be hindering your prayers? If so, confess to God and thank him for his promised forgiveness.

TALK TO OTHERS. Ask a trusted friend to pray with you about one of your current trials.

82. Grow in Assurance of Your Salvation

Therefore, brothers and sisters, be all the more diligent to confirm your calling and election, for if you practice these qualities you will never fall. For in this way there will be richly provided for you an entrance into the eternal kingdom of our Lord and Savior Jesus Christ. (2 Peter 1:10–11)

"Once saved, always saved" is a biblical doctrine. Yet the confidence it engenders is not without qualification. What do I mean? Repeatedly over the course of this book, we've seen from Scripture that the rescue of sinners such as ourselves should be credited completely to the triune God and not to ourselves. The Father planned it. The Son paid the required price. And the Spirit applied the life-giving gospel to our blinded eyes, deafened ears, and dulled wills. The triune God "brought us forth by the word of truth" (James 1:18). This implanted gospel seed produces life that continues to grow and bear fruit for him. However, we are not passive in this development. In the couple of verses before today's passage, Peter explains two blessings of growth.

Assurance of salvation. Certainty that you have been saved does not come from being able to remember when you made a decision, prayed a prayer, or walked an aisle. You "confirm your calling and election" by being diligent to see to it that godly virtues "are yours and are increasing" in your current walk (2 Peter 1:8). This progress keeps "you from being ineffective or unfruitful in the knowledge of our Lord Jesus Christ" (v. 8).

The flipside is equally true: "Whoever lacks these qualities is so nearsighted that he is blind, having forgotten that he was cleansed from his former sins" (2 Peter 1:9). The easiest way to short-circuit your assurance of salvation is to remain in your sin. Jesus says, "So if the Son sets you free, you will be free indeed" (John 8:36). Now walk in your freedom.

A triumphant future. The entrance of the fruitful believer into the eternal kingdom will be "richly provided." They will receive a "Well done, good servant!" (Luke 19:17) welcome rather than the loss of reward experienced by an unfruitful believer: "He himself will be saved, but only as through fire" (1 Cor. 3:15).

Don't misunderstand. In both cases, believers enter eternal life by grace alone, but the triumphant entry of the fruitful believer brings greater glory to God as the one who saves by grace, sanctifies by grace, and finally welcomes us home with a deluge of grace. This is the kind of welcome Paul must have anticipated: "I have fought the good fight, I have finished the race, I have kept the faith. Henceforth there is laid up for me the crown of righteousness" (2 Tim. 4:7–8).

Assurance of salvation grows in our hearts as we rest in the saving work of Jesus in our place, but it also grows in proportion to our progress with the Spirit who "bears witness with our spirit that we are children of God" (Rom. 8:16). For this reason, it's good for us to evaluate the fruit of our faith, as Paul exhorts us: "Examine yourselves, to see whether you are in the faith. Test yourselves" (2 Cor. 13:5).

Nevertheless, self-evaluation becomes unhealthy when it turns into morbid introspection. D. Martyn Lloyd-Jones warns of this in his classic book *Spiritual Depression*: "We cross the line from self-examination to introspection when, in a sense, we do nothing but examine ourselves, and when such self-examination becomes the main and chief end in our life. . . . If we are always doing it, always, as it were, putting our soul on a plate and dissecting it, that is introspection."[2] If we look inward too much, we will get stuck.

Ultimately, we look to Christ. In doing so, however, we look not only to his work on the cross in the past but also to heaven's throne room where our ascended High Priest now intercedes for us. We must look to the One "who is able to keep [us] from stumbling and to present [us] blameless before the presence of his glory with great joy, to the only God, our Savior, through Jesus Christ our Lord, be glory, majesty, dominion, and authority, before all time and now and forever. Amen" (Jude 24–25).

TALK TO YOURSELF. Read 1 Corinthians 11:17–34. Notice that one of the purposes of the Lord's Supper is to nudge us to examine ourselves. Do you do this regularly—perhaps the evening before you partake?

---

2. D. Martyn Lloyd-Jones, *Spiritual Depression: Its Causes and Cure* (Grand Rapids: Wm. B. Eerdmans, 1965), 17.

TALK TO GOD. Journal a prayer of thanksgiving for your assurance of salvation, which the Spirit develops in your heart as you grow in Christ and rest in his grace.

TALK TO OTHERS. Read 2 Peter 1:3–11 with a trustworthy believer who knows you well and discuss the Christian virtues listed there. Share the qualities in each other that you see progress in and point out ones that need attention. Pray for each other.

83. The Secret Things Belong to the Lord

The secret things belong to the LORD our God, but the things
that are revealed belong to us and to our children forever,
that we may do all the words of this law. (Deut. 29:29)

We often think that if we know more, we will worry less. For example, we may think that if we knew our nation's economy was going to be strong and flourishing ten years from now, we would worry less about our retirement. Perhaps. But we would worry about other things: our health, our child's or grandchild's education, and so on. We want to be like the God who has absolute knowledge of all things. The fact that we don't have absolute knowledge bothers us. It leads to anxiety, fear, and anger.

We feel our lack of complete knowledge acutely when we are taken off guard by a trial that we never saw coming, such as employment that ends prematurely, a marriage that dissolves, or a loved one who dies unexpectedly. Yet our lack of absolute knowledge is good news. We can be free from anxiety, fear, and anger because we belong to the God who does know all things. In the face of suffering and uncertainty, we cling to God and the truth he has given us to know. Today's verse teaches us three truths about God's revelation and what it means for us.

God keeps some things secret. The "secret things" that belong only to the Lord include the divine purposes behind his divine decrees. We seldom understand God's ways because he who created the universe is infinite and sovereign, which other Scriptures reveal. For example, he says, "I am God, and there is no other; I am God, and there is none like me, declaring the end from the beginning" (Isa. 46:9–10). Paul exclaims, "Oh, the depth of the riches and wisdom and knowledge of God! How unsearchable are his judgments and how inscrutable his ways!" (Rom. 11:33). God's thoughts and purposes are infinitely above our own (see Isa. 55:8–9), and that is good for us to know.

God has revealed what is necessary for you to know. Today's verse tells us that "the things that are revealed belong to us and to our children forever." Although there are some things you will never know, there is a great deal that you do know. Lay aside what you cannot understand and focus on what God has revealed in his Word. For example, you know God does only what is good (see Ps. 25:8) and holy (see Ps. 99:9) and right (see Ps. 145:17). You also know he strengthens you when you are afflicted (see Ps. 10:17).

God holds you accountable for how you respond to his revealed truth. Today's verse concludes that God reveals things to us "that we may do all the words of this law." God does not call you to understand the secret things that belong only to him. He only expects you to humbly respond in faith and obedience to what he has revealed in the Scriptures. Remembering that you are finite should take a lot of pressure off your shoulders.

When something happens that we don't understand, we have a choice to make. We may demand to know the secret things, doubt God, or perhaps even become angry and bitter against him. Or we may accept that our understanding is limited and trust him. We do not know everything, but we do know we have a God who can be trusted to make no mistakes. He is holy and righteous and good, and in this we may rejoice.

TALK TO YOURSELF. Read Psalm 46. In your journal, list the characteristics, imagery, and actions of God that bring you comfort.

TALK TO GOD. Pray through Psalm 46. Make it personal by inserting the first-person pronouns *I*, *me*, and *my*. For example, "God is *my* refuge and strength, a very present help in trouble" (v. 1).

TALK TO OTHERS. Do you know a fellow believer in Christ who is enduring an inexplicable season of suffering? Consider reading this chapter to them and then discuss the comfort that comes to us when we entrust our trials to the One who knows all things.

84. Resurrection Power through Suffering

. . . that I may know him and the power of his resurrection, and may share his sufferings, becoming like him in his death, that by any means possible I may attain the resurrection from the dead. (Phil. 3:10–11)

Eternal life is not primarily about going to heaven when we die. It's about having a relationship with God that begins in the here and now and continues forever. This is how Jesus defines it in John 17:3: "This is eternal life, that they know you, the only true God, and Jesus Christ whom you have sent." If eternal life is knowing God, and this life can be found only in the Son of God, then we must know Jesus (see 1 John 5:11–13). But is knowing Christ a one-time event or a lifelong process? Well, it's both. The apostle Paul explains this in Philippians 3:3–11.

Knowing Christ is a one-time event. To know the Lord, you must come to the same understanding that Paul did. That is, you must see yourself as a hopelessly lost sinner who deserves eternal death. You must then lay aside any "confidence in the flesh" or efforts at self-atonement or hopes of ever making yourself blameless (see Phil. 3:3; see also vv. 4–6). Like Paul, you must not trust in your works of righteousness but instead count them all "as loss for the sake of Christ" (v. 7).

When you exchange believing in yourself for resting in Jesus, you can say with Paul, "I count everything as loss because of the surpassing worth of knowing Christ Jesus my Lord. For his sake I have suffered the loss of all things and count them as rubbish, in order that I may gain Christ and be found in him, not having a righteousness of my own that comes from the law, but that which comes through faith in Christ" (3:8–9). This is what it means to know Christ: to exchange any sense of self-righteousness for the grace-gift of righteousness received in him.

Knowing Christ is a lifelong process. The relationship with Christ that begins at conversion should deepen as you get to know him practically. That is the overarching theme of this book. What might surprise you, however, is *the way* Paul wants to know Christ: by "shar[ing] his sufferings." In today's verses, the zealous persecutor-turned-apostle reveals his discontent with simply knowing Christ in a saving way—that is, merely knowing his sins are forgiven. He yearns to know him more deeply. James Montgomery Boice explains, "Paul wanted to know Jesus in the truest biblical sense—personally and experientially. And he wanted this to affect his day-by-day living."[3] This, Paul knew, was possible only if he was willing to associate with Christ in the dark valley of suffering.

Suffering contains the potential to grow us beyond what we typically think is possible, as we noticed in previous readings. But today it is crucial for us to think about how sharing in "his sufferings" helps us to know—and experience—the resurrection power of Christ.

In today's verses, the phrase "becoming like him in his death" is sandwiched between two phrases about resurrection life: "that I may know him and the power of his resurrection" and "that by any means possible I may attain the resurrection from the dead." Quite simply, the prerequisite to resurrection is death. It is illogical to crave resurrection power without also acknowledging that, to experience it, we must first die.

Paul knew this was the case and was prepared to suffer whatever God determined was necessary. He wanted to die to himself so that the resurrection power of Christ could be put on display through him. Is this the way you desire to know Jesus?

TALK TO YOURSELF. Prior to today's reading, what did the phrase *knowing Christ* mean to you? Read Paul's conversion story in Acts 25:24–26:29. In what ways is your story like his? In what ways is it different?

TALK TO GOD. Pray through Philippians 3:7–11.

3. James Montgomery Boice, *Philippians: An Expositional Commentary* (repr., Grand Rapids: Baker Books, 2000), 185.

TALK TO OTHERS. Ask a mature Christian or two to share with you how their experiences of suffering have helped them to know Christ more deeply.

85. Manifesting Life in Christ

For we who live are always being given over to death for Jesus' sake, so that the life of Jesus also may be manifested in our mortal flesh. (2 Cor. 4:11)

Christians are "jars of clay"; we are weak vessels who experience many afflictions of both body and spirit. But within our mortal frames dwells the hope found only in Jesus. As we learned in part 1 of this book, when we embrace Christ in the gospel, we are forever united to him and his Spirit takes up residence within us. Never is this more real to us than when we suffer. By the Spirit's power, "the life of Jesus" is made more visible in us, especially in times of trial.

Properly understood, suffering is a foretaste of death that draws attention to the only true source of life: Jesus. In 2 Corinthians 4:8–10, the larger context of today's verse, Paul describes the suffering that he and his coworkers experienced, which opens three windows through which we may look at our trials.

You may be "afflicted in every way, but not crushed" (4:8). Like followers of Jesus in the past, you are under pressure but, because of the life of Christ within you, you are not crushed or trapped. You may be "perplexed"—that is, at a loss or in doubt—but the Spirit will hold you to biblical hope, and you will not be despondent to the final point of despair. The life-giving Jesus keeps your hope alive.

You may be "persecuted, but not forsaken" (4:9). The word *persecuted* means to be hunted down like an animal. If you ever feel as if you are prey being chased down by trials, you need to remember this: although you may feel forgotten by others, the Lord "will never leave you nor forsake you" (Heb. 13:5).

You may be "struck down," but you won't be "destroyed" (2 Cor. 4:9). The word translated "struck down" means thrown down, as in a wrestling match. Numerous times this happened to the apostle Paul. At times, he was beaten and left for dead. But he was not destroyed; he did not perish. Like Paul, you can be assured that you will not die one minute earlier than God has destined for you. From beginning to end, your life is in God's hands (see Ps. 139:16).

Why did God ordain suffering for Paul and his companions and, in a similar way, for you and me? The apostle gives a surprising answer: so that we would trust not in ourselves but in "God who raises the dead" (2 Cor. 1:9). God ordains weakness and suffering so that we will trust not in ourselves but in him alone. Suffering might feel like death, but in God's economy it produces life.

God gives greater grace to us when we suffer. He gives grace when we need it the most. "For we who live are always being given over to death for Jesus' sake, so that the life of Jesus also may be manifested in our mortal flesh." In our weakness, we slowly walk to the executioner's stand so that self may die and the life of Jesus may be manifested in our mortal flesh. Our suffering is a foretaste of death that draws attention to the only source of true life: Jesus.

TALK TO YOURSELF. Say to yourself, "Yes, I may be thrown down by the trials of life, but in Christ, I am assured that I will not be ultimately destroyed. I am safe and secure with my Savior."

TALK TO GOD. Admit how weak and utterly spent suffering sometimes makes you feel. Ask God to use your suffering to put your self-life to death so that Christ is magnified in your mortal flesh.

TALK TO OTHERS. Ask a mature believer to share how their experience with weakness amidst suffering opened doors to conversation with those who saw how they were being strengthened by grace.

FUELED BY FAITH AND HOPE

86. "I Will Hope in Him"

*Though he slay me, I will hope in him; yet I will argue my
ways to his face. (Job 13:15)*

What can possibly move a man of faith to boldly proclaim his
undying devotion to the Lord even when that same Lord takes
away almost everything he gave? What could drive a man to surrender to the God who—in the space of one day—took away his
wealth, his property, and all ten of his children? Is it great faith?
Or is it simple faith in a great God who always keeps his word?

The testimony of the Old Testament patriarch Job argues for
the latter. Simple, bare-bones, gritty faith kept Job going. It's what
fueled his hope. When unthinkable torrents of pain collided with
his personal world, still he knew his standing before God was
secure. He kept his footing by remaining firmly planted on what
God said was true of himself.

Contrary to what we sometimes think, the book of Job is not
mainly about one man and his suffering. Instead, it's about the
rock-solid character of the sovereign God who is trustworthy
even when we experience tragedy beyond our comprehension.
Christopher Ash accurately points out that "the book of Job is

about true worship, about our bowing down in reality and in the darkness to the One who is God, leaving even our most agonizing unanswered questions at his feet, for we are creatures, and he alone is Creator."[1] Job's immediate response to his dreadful news is to worship: "Naked I came from my mother's womb, and naked shall I return. The LORD gave, and the LORD has taken away; blessed be the name of the LORD" (Job 1:21).

Job did not believe he was sinless. Instead, he recognized that he needed to be justified by God, and this led him to revere God. Job was "upright, one who feared God and turned away from evil" (1:1). He also knew that sin had to be atoned for, which explains why he regularly offered sacrifices on behalf of his children (see v. 5). Job's practice flowed from simple trust in the promise-keeping God who forgives.

The same must be true for us. Hope in times of intense suffering doesn't stem from being able to convince ourselves that we don't deserve what we're going through, that somehow we're getting a bum rap. The book of Job is an argument against self-justification.

Today's verse demonstrates Job's deep-seated confidence in God alone as "the justifier" of all who come to him by faith (see Rom. 3:26). Job's experience shattered the false worldview of his moralistic friends, who believed that bad things happen only to bad people and only good things happen to good people. Forced into a corner by the whitewashed lies of these "worthless physicians" of the soul (Job 13:4), Job is compelled to bring his case before God. Even if God should "slay" him for it, Job has no one else to turn to except his Creator and Redeemer and therefore affirms, "I will hope in him" (v. 15). God, not himself, is Job's defense.

Like Job, we need to remind ourselves that our standing before God is secure—that is, we have been justified by God and before

---

1. R. Albert Mohler Jr., ed., *The Grace and Truth Study Bible* (Grand Rapids: Zondervan, 2021), 643.

God through our faith in Christ. We sustain our hope as we grip God with what little strength we have *while* knowing that what matters in the end is that he is gripping us.

TALK TO YOURSELF. Read Job 1:1–22. If you were enduring the same circumstances as Job, do you think your response to your suffering would resemble his? Why or why not?

TALK TO GOD. Confess any faithless responses to your past or current trials. Ask God to help you to grow in simple, gritty faith in his sovereign care.

TALK TO OTHERS. Is there anyone in your life who is going through an unthinkable trial right now? How can you encourage them with Christ-centered hope, rather than heaping a burden of moralism onto their already weak shoulders?

87. God's Bigger and Better Plan

As for you, you meant evil against me, but God meant it for good, to bring it about that many people should be kept alive, as they are today. (Gen. 50:20)

When trials come, it's easy for us to wonder if God is really in control or if he can bring good out of the bad things that happen to us. Scripture allows us to see suffering from God's vantage point, but this doesn't mean all our questions will be answered. Yet it does mean we may be confident that God will work on behalf of those whom he loves. He is always up to something good as he works out a bigger and better plan than we can imagine.

Spoken by one who endured many kinds of suffering, today's Scripture reading is a great source of hope for us. Joseph faced his share of trouble. Yet his life was filled with dramatic and obvious displays of divine providence. A sermon in the book of Acts provides a fitting summary of Joseph's purposeful suffering (see Acts 7:9–14).

Stephen, a leader of the church in Jerusalem, was hauled before the authorities and falsely accused. Instead of turning inward, he seized the opportunity to preach a long view of redemption. He reminded his listeners of God's rescue of the Hebrew people throughout the Old Testament and how God preserved the hope of salvation for all mankind through Joseph's suffering. In both the trials and triumphs of Joseph, we see God's gospel unfold in a beautiful tapestry of grace. Two beautiful threads are woven through this tapestry that can encourage you in times of trial.

God's providence assures you of his presence. Joseph's trials began when he was seventeen years old, after he brought a bad report about his brothers to their dad (see Gen. 37:1–4). This, along with his father's display of favoritism and Joseph's dreams of future greatness, provoked his brothers to jealous hatred. They sold him into slavery in a foreign land. Falsely accused by his master's wife, Joseph soon found himself in prison, where he may have been tempted to think that God had forgotten him (see 37:21–35; 39:19–20). But that was not the case. Repeatedly, Scripture assures us that "the LORD was with Joseph" (see 39:2–3, 21–23). At every moment, God was compassionately attentive to his servant. The same is true for you in your suffering.

God's providence includes redemptive purposes. Twenty-two years after Joseph's brothers betrayed him, the Lord used a famine to bring them to Egypt to buy grain. Although they interacted several times, Joseph did not reveal his identity until an emotional dam broke. The floodgates of Joseph's heart opened before his abusers and he drew them near, saying, "I am your brother, Joseph, whom you sold into Egypt. And now do not be distressed or angry with yourselves because you sold me here, for God sent me before you to preserve life" (Gen. 45:5). God had a bigger and better plan for Joseph's pain, which included the redemption of many. The same may be true for you in your suffering.

When inexplicable suffering enters our lives, we can rest assured that God has not stepped away from his throne. No, he is still sovereign, and he is present with us. He walks through our valleys with us and leads us toward the fulfillment of his good and perfect will.

TALK TO YOURSELF. How have you seen the invisible hand of God's providence at work for good in your life?

TALK TO GOD. Write a prayer of thanksgiving that reflects your trust in God for his faithful providence.

TALK TO OTHERS. Ask a mature Christian to read Genesis 37–50 with you. Talk about the ways the Lord was "with Joseph" throughout his trials and about how this applies to you both.

88. The Crown of Life

*Count it all joy, my brothers and sisters, when you meet
trials of various kinds, for you know that the testing of your
faith produces steadfastness. And let steadfastness have its
full effect, that you may be perfect and complete, lacking in
nothing. . . . Blessed is the man who remains steadfast under
trial, for when he has stood the test he will receive the crown
of life, which God has promised to those who love him.*
(James 1:2–4, 12)

On a shelf in my home office, there is a brass clock engraved with
the words *Volunteer of the Year, 1998*. I received the clock for serving as a hospice chaplain with the Visiting Nurse Association of
Wisconsin. I attended to patients and their families because the
Holy Spirit placed the ministry of comfort on my heart. The pastor
in me longed for people in their final days to know that Jesus will
save any sinner who, like the repentant thief on the cross, looks to
him with humble, childlike faith (see Luke 23:43). I would have
kept serving as the Lord called me, with or without a reward.
Nevertheless, it was meaningful to me to be appreciated. I'm
guessing the same may be true of you.

Scripture mentions various heavenly rewards that are promised
to faithful Christians: an imperishable prize to those who finish
the race (see 1 Cor. 9:24–25), a heavenly inheritance to those who
work "heartily, as for the Lord and not for men" (Col. 3:23; see
also v. 24), the crown of righteousness to those who look to Jesus's
coming (see 2 Tim. 4:8), an unnamed reward for all those who
build their ministry on the foundation of Christ (see 1 Cor. 3:14),
and a crown of glory to faithful church shepherds (see 1 Peter 5:4).
Earthly rewards may be a powerful incentive for some to exhibit
faithfulness, but how much more should believers be motivated
by everlasting rewards!

Today's Scripture reading names another reward that you may find encouraging when your endurance wanes. The "crown of life" is God's promise to you for remaining "steadfast under trial." When your faith has "stood the test" of trials and persecution, James says you will not be forgotten. You will be remembered by the One who matters most.

The person who lives for earthly riches and rewards will glory only "in his humiliation, because like a flower of the grass he will pass away" (James 1:10). He will "fade away in the midst of his pursuits" (v. 11). But those who persevere in faith prove the genuineness of their faith, for which they will receive a reward "which God has promised to those who love him."

Promised rewards are a way that God encourages us. As we remain steadfast through whatever trials come our way, the Spirit authenticates our faith—he confirms it to the end. Having this eternal perspective helps us to "consider that the sufferings of this present time are not worth comparing with the glory that is to be revealed" (Rom. 8:18), and to count it joy "when [we] meet trials of various kinds, for [we] know that the testing of [our] faith produces steadfastness."

TALK TO YOURSELF. Have you ever thought about any of God's promised rewards? If so, how has it affected your walk with him?

TALK TO GOD. Read Matthew 7:7–11. Write a prayer of appreciation for God's generosity toward his children.

TALK TO OTHERS. Are any of your brothers or sisters in the Lord going through a time of severe testing? Send them a note or text reminding them of the goodness of the heavenly Father.

89. Embrace the Christ-Centered Life

*If then you have been raised with Christ, seek the things that
are above, where Christ is, seated at the right hand of God.
(Col. 3:1)*

In December 2012, children discovered the body of a homeless
man who had frozen to death under a railroad bridge in Wyoming.
Soon after, he was identified as Timothy Gray, a long-lost relative
of a reclusive heiress who had left him $19 million of her $300
million fortune.[2] Sadly, some Christians live in a similar manner.
Although we are indescribably wealthy in Christ, we sometimes
live like we don't know that we will soon inherit an eternal home.

Colossians 3, where we find today's verse, marks a decisive shift
in the book: from doctrine to living, from theology to practice. In
Colossians 1 and 2, the apostle expresses pastoral concern over
disciples who are beginning to follow worldly philosophies and
erroneous religious regulations rather than Christ. He charges his
readers to rearrange their lives so that every part revolves around
the true center—the Lord Jesus. Just as every planet in our solar
system revolves around the sun, so every aspect of our lives should
revolve around the Son of God. Jesus should be the center of all!

The word *if* that opens today's verse may also be translated
"since." In other words, *because* this is true, that "you have been

---

2. Carey Vanderborg, "Homeless Heir Timothy Henry Gray Stood to Inherit
Fortune of Huguette Clark, New York Railroad Heiress," *International Business
Times,* December 31, 2012, https://www.ibtimes.com/homeless-heir-timothy
-henry-gray-stood-inherit-fortune-huguette-clark-new-york-railroad-heiress.

raised with Christ," *then* do this: "Seek the things that are above, where Christ is, seated at the right hand of God." You are already seated "with him in the heavenly places" (Eph. 2:6). *Positionally*, Jesus is already the center of your life. Now, *practically*, you need to realign everything in your personal solar system to revolve around him. How do you do this?

Give attention to Christ-centered living. In the Greek, the word *seek* implies continual action. In this way, Paul draws attention to your responsibility to stay on course, to pursue "the things that are above." To do so, you must set "your minds on things that are above, not on things that are on earth" (Col. 3:2). This requires vigilance since we live in a world that is filled with so many distractions and temptations. It's easy to lose our proper focus and for life to become blurry.

Live in the light of who you already are. The reason you should keep seeking Christ is logical: "You have died" (Col. 3:3). God already sees you as "dead to sin and alive to God in Christ Jesus" (Rom. 6:11). In Christ, the power of sin in you has already been broken. You don't have to live under its dominion anymore.

And, if this isn't reason enough, the apostle continues, "Your life is hidden with Christ in God" (Col. 3:3). The word *hidden* implies an unseen place of security and safety. Unlike the things of the world, the life you have in Christ is not visible to you. It's a walk of faith. But what a comfort to know that no matter what dangers you may face along the pathway of life, nothing can ultimately touch you unless God wills it to be so. And you have the assurance of a safe and secure future: "When Christ who is your life appears, then you also will appear with him in glory" (v. 4).

We should not live as though we are spiritually poor and homeless. In Christ, we have all that we need and much, much more. In him, we possess all the spiritual riches and privileges that come with being adopted children of God and joint heirs with the Son of God.

TALK TO YOURSELF. Read Philippians 3:12–16. Journal about how Paul moved forward in his pursuit of Christ and how he describes spiritual maturity. Look for ways this exercise can renew your mind and energize your walk with Christ.

TALK TO GOD. Review the list you made and write a prayer that expresses your own spiritual longing to grow in your pursuit of Christ.

TALK TO OTHERS. In your time in Philippians 3:12–16, did you notice Paul's use of the plural pronoun "us" in verses 15–16? Have you taken intentional steps to pursue Christ in the company of others? How can you and other believers help one another to make progress in your spiritual walk?

CONCLUSION

90. Reside in Gospel Reality

*I have been crucified with Christ; and it is no longer I who
live, but Christ lives in me; and the life which I now live in
the flesh I live by faith in the Son of God, who loved me and
gave Himself up for me. (Gal. 2:20 NASB)*

Keeping the main thing the main thing is difficult, but it's essential
to living the Christ-centered life. The apostle's confession of faith
in today's verse is an example. It testifies to a profound spiritual
reality: every sinner-turned-saint, every believer justified by God
through their faith in Jesus alone, is now in spiritual union with
Christ. Our old self (who we were in Adam) has been crucified
with Jesus. And, by faith in the resurrected Christ, we have been
raised to new life. The Spirit of Christ now indwells us, and the
life of Christ is now being lived out through us. Jesus is now the
center of everything. He is our true north.

The core purpose of your life has changed. There's been a seis-
mic shift in your heart's posture toward God and godliness. When
the Spirit brought you to life, he began to reorient your desires to
worship Christ, to renew your thoughts by the pure water of his
Word, and to replace your habits with new patterns of godliness.

All these changes take place as you traverse hills, valleys, and unexpected twists and turns. Your journey will continue until you meet Jesus face-to-face. This is what it means to reside in the reality of *who* you are, and *whose* you are, and *who* you are becoming like—Jesus. This means you need to keep Christ central by living in the reality of two gospel truths.

Your old self is dead, but your new self is alive unto God. "Christ lives in me," the apostle shouts. Remember that "you have died, and your life is hidden with Christ in God" (Col. 3:3). In your former life you were wrapped up in pleasing yourself, but now you see and reflect the glory of your Savior. Everything is different. So, when you get stuck in the weeds and your spiritual garden doesn't seem to be flourishing, reside in this gospel reality: at one time you were dead to God, but now you are dead to sin and alive unto God. Keep walking in your new life and, in time, your fruit will increase.

The Christian life works itself out in a walk of faith. Like Paul, you can say, "The life which I now live in the flesh I live by faith in the Son of God." Remember, you are justified by faith, and you live by faith. Walking with Christ requires abiding in him and his Word (see John 15:7). You need to stay close to your Savior.

A warm, joyful, and intimate relationship with Christ doesn't just happen. It must be cultivated by reflecting on his love, especially the love he displayed on the cross. Remember your rescue, but remember your Savior's present work too. He is "at the right hand of God," where he is currently "interceding" for you (Rom. 8:34). Stoke the flames of your love for Jesus by letting "the word of Christ dwell in you richly" (Col. 3:16). Warm your heart at the fire of biblical meditation.

In Christ, you are traveling down Sanctification Road. Along the way, you face the temptation to return to the pleasure of sin, while also encountering the pain of suffering. Both challenges test your faith and provide opportunities to stimulate your growth in Christ as you remember who you are. You are in Christ, and Christ is in you. Immerse yourself in the living and powerful Word of God, for there you will behold the One in whose image you are being remade.

TALK TO YOURSELF. Memorize Galatians 2:20. Write it on a 3 x 5 card or type it into a note in your smartphone. Review it regularly to remind yourself of your identity in Christ and the good work the Spirit is doing within you.

TALK TO GOD. In your journal, write out a three-part prayer to God. First, thank him for his gracious gospel work within you, which made you a *saint*. Second, ask the Spirit to help you to apply your new identity in Christ to your daily struggles as a saint who still, at times, thinks and behaves like a *sinner*. Third, thank God for his good purposes in your trials. As a *sufferer*, ask him to cause you to grow in humility as you submit to the purifying power of trials and testing.

TALK TO OTHERS. Consider reading through this book again, this time with another believer. One way to do this would be to read through each five-chapter section separately and then get together over coffee to talk about what you are learning. Once you've finished this book, try out one of the books from the recommended reading section that follows.

RECOMMENDED READING

ON PROGRESSIVE SANCTIFICATION

Bridges, Jerry. *Transforming Grace*. New ed. Colorado Springs: NavPress, 2017.

Ferguson, Sinclair B. *The Whole Christ: Legalism, Antinomianism, and Gospel Assurance: Why the Marrow Controversy Still Matters*. Wheaton, IL: Crossway, 2016.

Hedges, Brian G. *Christ Formed in You: The Power of the Gospel for Personal Change*. Wapwallopen, PA: Shepherd Press, 2010.

Newheiser, Jim. *Help! I Want to Change*. Wapwallopen, PA: Shepherd Press, 2014.

Powlison, David. *How Does Sanctification Work?* Wheaton, IL: Crossway, 2017.

Tiffe, Armand P. *Transformed Into His Likeness: A Handbook for Putting Off Sin and Putting on Righteousness*. Bemidji, MN: Focus Publishing, 2015.

Vincent, Milton. *A Gospel Primer for Christians: Learning to See the Glories of God's Love*. Bemidji, MN: Focus Publishing, 2008.

ON OVERCOMING TEMPTATION

Adams, Jay E. *Temptation: Applying Radical Amputation to Life's Sinful Patterns*. Phillipsburg, NJ: P&R Publishing, 2012.

Hedges, Brian G. *Watchfulness: Recovering a Lost Spiritual Discipline*. Grand Rapids: Reformation Heritage Books, 2018.

Jones, Mark. *Knowing Sin: Seeing a Neglected Doctrine through the Eyes of the Puritans*. Chicago: Moody Publishers, 2022.

Lundgaard, Kris. *The Enemy Within: Straight Talk about the Power and Defeat of Sin*. Rev. ed. Phillipsburg, NJ: P&R Publishing, 2023.

Owen, John. *Temptation: Resisted and Repulsed*. Carlisle: Banner of Truth, 2021.

Saxton, David W. *God's Battle Plan for the Mind: The Puritan Practice of Biblical Meditation*. Grand Rapids: Reformation Heritage Books, 2015.

Tautges, Paul. *Bitterness: When You Can't Move On*. Greensboro, NC: New Growth Press, 2023.

ON ENDURING SUFFERING

Bridges, Jerry. *Trusting God*. Colorado Springs: NavPress, 1988.

Elliot, Elisabeth. *Suffering Is Never for Nothing*. Nashville: B&H Publishing, 2019.

James, Joel. *Help! I Can't Handle All These Trials*. Wapwallopen, PA: Shepherd Press, 2016.

Kress, Eric, and Paul Tautges. *God's Mercy in Our Suffering: Lamentations for Pastors and Counselors*. The Woodlands, TX: Kress Biblical Resources, 2019.

Powlison, David. *God's Grace in Your Suffering*. Wheaton, IL: Crossway, 2018.

Tada, Joni Eareckson, with Steven Estes. *When God Weeps: Why Our Sufferings Matter to the Almighty*. Grand Rapids: Zondervan, 2020.

Tautges, Paul, with Joni Eareckson Tada. *When Disability Hits Home: How God Magnifies His Grace in Our Weakness and Suffering*. Wapwallopen, PA: Shepherd Press, 2020.

Tripp, Paul David. *A Shelter in the Time of Storm: Meditation on God and Trouble*. Wheaton, IL: Crossway, 2009.

Vroegop, Mark. *Dark Clouds, Deep Mercy: Discovering the Grace of Lament*. Wheaton, IL: Crossway Books, 2019.

ABOUT THE COVER

For hundreds of years, Japanese artists have repaired valuable pottery by sealing the breaks with a lacquer mixed with powdered gold. The word for this tradition, *kintsugi*, comes from the Japanese *kin* ("gold") and *tsugi* ("join") and literally means "to join with gold."

Joni Eareckson Tada first introduced me to this art form in reference to the dignity of people with disabilities. She explained, "Rather than trashing a shattered ceramic jar—tossing it aside because it is worthless—the artists carefully gather the broken shards and use the lacquered gold substance to adhere them back together. The gold is an agent that creates a stunning work of art, resulting in a jar not only that is more lovely but that has a redemptive story." Joni related kintsugi to our redemption in Christ: God picks us up and applies the gold of his grace to our brokenness—not disguising it but putting his grace on display for all to see.

As the publisher and I brainstormed potential cover concepts for this book, the image of kintsugi returned to my mind. Our lives are damaged and broken by humanity's sin and our own personal rebellion. But God, the ultimate artist, intervenes. He picks up the broken pieces, redeems and forgives us, and joins us to Jesus as we have faith in him. The Spirit frees us from the power of sin and employs suffering to sanctify our hearts and refine our faith, which is "more precious than gold" (1 Peter 1:7). In Christ, we are reborn, redeemed, and remade into the image of the one who saves us, and our lives become a beautiful testimony to our glorious Savior. All glory be to Christ!

From P&R and the
Biblical Counseling Coalition

MEGAN HILL

PAUL TAUTGES

MEGAN HILL

ROBERT D. JONES

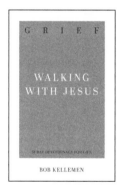

BOB KELLEMEN

ESTHER LIU

In the 31-Day Devotionals for Life series, biblical counselors and Bible teachers guide you through Scripture passages that speak to specific situations or struggles, helping you to apply God's Word to your life in practical ways day after day.

Devotionals endorsed by Brad Bigney, Kevin Carson, Mark Dever, John Freeman, Gloria Furman, Melissa Kruger, Mark Shaw, Winston Smith, Joni Eareckson Tada, Ed Welch, and more!

Did you find this book helpful?
Consider writing a review online.
We appreciate your feedback!

Or write to P&R at editorial@prpbooks.com
with your comments. We'd love to hear from you.